The Wright Brothers

Flight is Possible

a novel

by

John Passfield

Rock's Mills Press
Oakville, Ontario
2020

Published by
Rock's Mills Press
www.rocksmillspress.com

© 2006, 2020 by John Passfield. All rights reserved.

No part of this book may be reproduced, stored in a retrieval system, or transmitted by any means without the written permission of the author.

An earlier edition of this novel first appeared in 2006. Minor changes have been incorporated in this new edition.

Cover Images: Library of Congress, U.S. Air Force archives

Cover Design: Craig Passfield

Author's website: www.johnpassfield.ca

Chapter 1
The Wright Brothers 1

Kitty Hawk, North Carolina
December 17, 1903

Morning at Kitty Hawk. Thursday, December 17th, 1903. Today, perhaps, is the day that we will fly. Much later, by a couple of months, than we ever thought we'd be. Bad weather too. Clear and cold isn't too bad, but listen to that wind. Coming from the north. Must be twenty or twenty-five miles an hour, at least. The roar of the waves as they break on the shore. The ocean is angry today. The wind must be thirty miles an hour off-shore to make those waves. And coming from the north means it's extra cold.

Prometheus was torn and bleeding. He brushed aside the brambles and stumbled on loose rock. There was no moonlight to alleviate the darkness, but he knew where there was a glow that could be seen.

Very seldom did he venture out in the dark.

He could not see past his elbows. He held his hands out to protect his eyes. The brambles slashed and scratched him, but he stumbled and grunted on. He was determined to get to a spot where he knew he would be able to see the distant glow.

How will man fly? Will his wings flap or glide? How is he to steer? How will he stay stable in the air? What will power this strange machine that he seeks to invent? What will propel this machine forward through the air?

If man is ever going to fly, it must be by a process of problem-theory-test-and-solution, not of trial-and-error. Trial-and-error is a process that has been followed for a hundred years. It is a process that, so far, has not been successful. To build a set of wings on a guess and hope that the strange machine will fly is a great mistake. To build and test two hundred wings, for instance, one summer at a time, would obviously take two hundred years.

Octave Chanute left Kitty Hawk a month ago. After forty years of yearning for man to rise above the earth and fly, he complained that Kitty Hawk in December would be far too cold for him to stay.

He went home to where he could sit and read by the fire.

December 1903. The Seventeenth day of December. A cold day at Kitty Hawk, with winter coming on. Strong winds and cold air. Ice on the puddles and a crust on top of the sand. Dampness seeping into the blankets and the clothes.

The attempt to fly is certainly important, but Christmas is approaching. A difficult choice to make, perhaps, but we are determined that we will do both: be the first human beings to fly, and do it in time to spend Christmas Day at home.

Data, technical terms, numbers, equations. The water we swim in; the air we breathe. An envelope of creativity that surrounds us. A cloud of terminology. A mist of numbers, theories and concepts that we breathe into our lungs and into our bloodstream. The element that we live in; the element in which we will continue to live until we have mastered the age-old secret of human flight.

Pitch and yaw and roll - rise and fall of nose and tail - degree of turn about a vertical axis - turn about a longitudinal axis - wind tests - centre-of-pressure - light winds - stronger winds - centre of gravity - how do birds manage to change the shape of their wings?

Leonardo was up at dawn. As soon as the sun came through the window, he would rise. No sense lying awake and thinking. He could never see sense in that. He would soon think of something and throw the cover back and swing his legs out onto the floor and reach for his notebook to record the fleeting thought.

Thoughts came, in particular detail, only once. Over the days and months and years, they would return many times, in an effort to refine themselves, but a particular version could be captured only once.

The first problem, as we have come to understand it, is one of lateral balance. How does a bird stay stable in the wind? If a bird is jostled off-balance – when a bird is blown off-course – what does it do to correct its flight and regain its stability?

Drift - net drift-lift - head resistance - false lift - airfoil profile - edge resistance - resultant pressure - total resistance - tangential measuring machine - frame of the balance.

The rain is frozen in the puddles of the sand-hollows. The sand is pocked with rain-drop tracks. Just a few gulls out over the water. The waves are smashing on the beach. Putting firewood into the stove. Taking the poker and stoking the embers. We split the oak stumps up just a few days ago. Father's lesson on slabbing came in handy once again. Won't be long and we'll have ourselves a little more heat.

Home. Heart and hearth. Home is warm bread and clean socks. Fresh laundry and sand-free sheets. Home is Father – Pop – sitting by the fireplace reading over the church reports, slashing with an angry pencil, working up ammunition for his on-going battle with the council of the Church of The United Brethren of Christ.

Home is Katharine – Schwesterchen – at her desk in the parlour, working on her lessons in Ancient History, books spread out in front of her, turning to share a titbit –

peering over her glasses at her brothers, Ullam and Bubs, who are sprawled on the sofa – telling tales of the days of the antique gods. Filling in the pauses in our discussions about drift and head resistance and resultant pressure. Telling stories of Prometheus and Olympus, of Icarus and Daedelus, of Phaeton and the Chariot of the Sun. Things that she thinks we might like to know about the ancient and persistent dream of human flight. Tales that take us to the library to load up on books about the Greek Myths and the drawings of Leonardo.

How does a bird maintain stability? And how will a man – who is not a bird – maintain stability in the air? The others have not considered this. The others have made great strides, but have also gone wrong. They want to create a fixed system so that a machine will fly itself through the air, ploughing through the clouds and never flinching.

But this approach is wrong. The flying machine cannot fly itself. It is man who must learn to control the flying machine. He must glide until he has learned to respond to the wind.

Head resistance - surface in equilibrium - curvature - horizontal elevator - 17 miles an hour - Richard's anemometer - 240 lbs. - angle of incidence - three degrees - one hundred pounds.

Coffee on the stove. Getting dressed. Ice on the surface of the washbasin. A little help from the carbide-can stove. A wash and a shave. Pants, suit jacket, collar and tie. Today might be a picture-taking day. Shoulder against the door. Stepping outside. The wind is like a wall that presses against you. Not much chance of flying in this. The anemometer showing a little over twenty miles per hour. Maybe things will ease off a bit as the morning progresses. Nothing to do but watch the wind and wait and see.

Swatting up in the library. Lugging a stack of library books home in a bag.

Just what do the Greeks imagine a flying man to be? Flapping wings? Fixed wings? The soar of an eagle? A buzzard-like glide? Leather harnesses? Feathers and paste? Does the air get thinner or thicker, colder or hotter, the higher a Greek mythological character flies?

Leonardo made his way through Florence. He paused, and shifted the bag that contained his notebook to his other shoulder. His limp was still with him, but today was no exception. In the past, he had never let it slow him down.

The buildings caught the glow of the early morning. Santa Maria Novella. San Marco. San Lorenzo. The Palace of the Medici. The Palazzo della Signoria. The church of Or San Michelle. The Baptistry. Bruneleschi's Dome. Giotto's Bell Tower.

Surely Florence was the nonpareil of all of the cities that he had known. Florence in the dawn has known no peer.

Man must control the machine. The machine, in turn, must be completely responsive to the man.

A man who rides a bicycle is like a man who is riding the air. The rider is always maintaining balance, making adjustments, correcting imbalances, every second, every moment, as he rides. If the rider relaxes control, the machine will fall.

Lifting capacity - calculated amount - porosity of the cloth - the lift of curved surfaces - true velocity - the Smeaton coefficient - 90 degrees - 20 percent - Lilienthal's estimates - 3 degrees.

Too cold to work outside. Shaking the sand out of the newspaper and sitting down to read with a cup of coffee.

It is all being covered in the newspapers. Our rivalry with the eminent Professor Langley. A race to put a manned and powered flying machine into the air.

Well, not all of it is being reported. The Professor Langley half of the rivalry is being well covered. Our own half of the rivalry remains unreported and completely unknown.

That is exactly the way we want it to continue.

A sip of coffee and a closer look. Smooth the newspaper out on the table and scan for the details of the flying machine that the professor claims will inaugurate human flight.

Back inside the shed. Rubbing our hands to get the blood flowing. Sand blowing in little spurts right through the cracks. If the wind picks up, it's going to be a gale. If the weather doesn't break, that will be the entire season. There won't be any more flying until next year. The water has dried and left a shallow trough in the sand. If we do try flight today, we could use that shallow trough for the laying of the launching-track.

Swatting up in the library. Winter nights spent reading by the fire.

And what of Leonardo? Just what exactly does Leonardo think? Just exactly what does Leonardo draw? How close does he actually come to understanding the basic principles that will govern a machine in which a man will be able to fly?

A man will not be shot through the air as if he is riding on an arrow.

A man rides a bicycle in different planes at once. The bicycle cannot possibly control itself. The man is constantly righting the bicycle – constantly adjusting its balance. When the bicycle leans over, the man is constantly applying control to regain equilibrium.

Surely flying machines will work on a similar principle.

Angle of descent - net drift - edge resistance - rectangular pressure - gliding angle - normal pressure - total resistance - head resistance - airfoil surface - propelling force.

We are at Kitty Hawk much later than we have ever stayed before. For this, we have to thank Professor Langley. Professor Langley can't possibly fly. We know that from the newspapers. We know that from our reading between the lines. We know too much about human flight to believe that he is anywhere near to achieving a successful experiment. And yet, blind luck might be a factor. Guess and trial might lead to something. Strides have been made by people who have guessed and guessed again. If we do not fly now, Professor Langley, with many thousands of dollars, and an army of worker bees, with a powerful, heavy motor and ridiculously unscientific wings, might just blunder into success. Might just become the first to achieve powered human flight.

Kitty Hawk is cold; home is warm. Kitty Hawk is damp; home is dry. Christmas is coming, but we are determined that we will do both: we will make the world's first flight, here at Kitty Hawk, North Carolina, and we will return home, to Dayton, Ohio and be with our father and our sister, Katharine, for Christmas.

Without family, as father says – about as often as he ever says anything else – you are alone.

We can only wonder about the departure of Octave Chanute.

Leonardo limped through the Piazza della Signoria.
Bustling with the noise of the morning trade. The sun and the shade moving together across the stones. Baskets and wines and cheeses and rope. Fish and fruit and meat and drink. Eyefuls of wool and silk and flax and exquisite dyes. A cascade of sounds and sights and gestures and pungent scents.
A loaf of bread, at Antonio's shop, to tuck in his pack. "Grazie, Antonio, grazie. This loaf of bread will be plenty enough for me."
The Ponte Vecchio, across the Arno, and out of town. Setting out on the path that leads to the hills.

We must not over-study the birds. Birds have been studied for thousands of years and man has not flown. We must develop a theory of how a man might control his wings. Only then might we learn by looking at the birds.
There are many kinds of birds. Birds that flap their wings in constant motion, and birds that glide for hours, and seem to make no moves at all – moves so subtle they cannot be detected by the human eye.
The others have had it all wrong. Their gliders have led us here, but for years they have repeated themselves with no advance. They have relied on body movement for control of their machines, but this method will never lead to control of the air. Man has limits and man has strengths. We must study man if man is ever to learn to fly.

Chord of the arc - .545 of the pressure - 50 percent greater - perpendicular - errors in the methods - errors, errors, errors - horizontal pressure - angles of incidence - 23 lbs. - 13 degrees.

Another cup of coffee and the flicking of the sand from the newspaper page. How far along is Professor Langley in his attempt to put a manned and powered flying machine into the air?

Man cannot control a flying machine with his body. It's a simple matter of thought: a machine which is large enough and strong enough to carry a man through the air could not respond to the man when the man starts shifting his weight. The machine would weigh more than the man. The machine would ignore the man and start to fall.
Man will need a system of control to make the machine respond to shifting conditions in the air. Perhaps the birds do move their wings when they are buffeted. If you think of what a man must do to regain control in the air, you can look at a bird through binoculars and start to believe that you can see what it is that the birds actually do. If a man lost his equilibrium, he would have to adjust his wings. Perhaps that is what the

birds do. Perhaps they compensate for the momentary loss of control by making subtle adjustments to the tips of their wings.

There must be a way to control the wings when a man is buffeted out of a stable position – a method of shifting the ends of the wings of a flying machine.

Head resistance - sine of 13 degrees - cosine of 13 degrees - average pressure - pressure on the surface - instability - straight-line glides - front elevator - the curvature of the wing - resistance to flight.

The Potomac River rolls behind the learned Professor.

"I do not know of anyone who has advanced the field of aeronautics as far as we have advanced it here, at our laboratory in Washington," Professor Langley tells the reporters who have gathered for the interview.

He waves his hand towards the Potomac. Towards the houseboat on the river. Towards the launching-rail on the roof. Towards the very spot in the river where the Langley Aerodrome will attempt the first powered human flight.

Prometheus had stood in front of Zeus that time. His feet were a little tender from the shale. It had been a long climb and the day was hot. He was being disciplined for having wandered into territory which had been forbidden.

Some of the gods had grumbled at having been called to an assembly, but Zeus had insisted that they be present to hear his word. The great Zeus did not take kindly to requests.

Zeus had stood in front of Prometheus and stared at him, hard, in the eyes.

"You will always be Man," Zeus had told him. "No matter where you go on earth, or what you do, or what you think – you will always be Man. You will be bound by all of the attributes of your earthliness."

Prometheus had clenched his teeth and folded his fists at his side and said nothing.

Fair enough, he thought, while looking Zeus in the eye, but being a Man, I think I know better than you can possibly know how far and wide those human bounds have been set. I think I know better than you can possibly know how far Mankind can reach and still be Man. I refuse to accept any limits to what Man can do.

The twisting of a box! The simple twisting of a box! That has to be the solution to the problem of control in human flight!

Talking to a customer in the bicycle shop while twisting a cardboard box! Such a very simple thing and such a major breakthrough! Birds can move their wing-tips, and now man will be able to do the same!

This is how a man can adjust his wings!

Angle of incidence - drift-lift ratio - gliding angle - resultant pressure - rectangular pressure - P 90 pressure - drift- tangential resistance - tangential difference - retarding force - tables of tangentials.

Glancing at each other. Too early yet to even think of making a decision. When the time comes to make the decision, we'll not only know the time, we'll know the decision. Professor Langley is preparing a machine. The winter is settling in. We have decided to spend Christmas at home. Conditions that are not completely wrong will have to be right. Enough fuel to fly about eight miles before the tank runs dry. That would be about eight miles straight in calm air. Not much chance of that today. Not much chance of flying anywhere today.

Kitty Hawk is cold and damp – especially now, in the middle of December; sand at the cracks and wind at the door – but there is never any sacrifice. Never any sense of being deprived in pursuit of success.

The Arctic explorers often waited out a year, and sometimes two, trapped in their ships, with the drinking water frozen and the fuel running low, battling scurvy and facing starvation, before the ice-pack would finally yield and let them through.

Kitty Hawk is cold and damp, but there was something else that hastened the departure of Octave Chanute.

For four seasons now – '00, '01, '02, '03 – we have always thought of our time at Kitty Hawk as being on vacation. Mosquitoes, sand and cold, perhaps, but also friends and the fresh sea breeze and the warming sun. Many setbacks, of course, but definitely, always, a steady advance.

When the left hand moves forward, and the right hand moves back, the box will twist. And so will the wings on the flying machine. The wings will twist – one up and one down. The wings will warp and there will be changes in the air pressure over and under each wing.

Shape of the wings - slipping sideways - five-foot span - lateral control - weight shifting - biplane configuration - the Pratt Truss - fore-and-aft diagonal bracing - crossed-wire system - wing-warping - across the chord.

Shaking the sand out of the newspaper once again.
Our rival, Professor Langley, is very confident.
"In this flying machine," Professor Langley tells the newspapers, "we have incorporated all of the advances made by all of the inventors who have tackled the age-old problem of human flight. We have here, in the Langley Aerodrome, as will shortly be demonstrated – to enthusiasts and sceptics alike – the most advanced flying machine that mankind has ever known."

There was a glow on Mount Olympus. Prometheus stood on a branch of a tree, hanging onto the trunk with a bear-hug, and gazed up onto the mountain, far away.
From here he could see what he had been thinking about for so long. There was a glow, despite the darkness, on the home of the gods.
That glow, he had been told, would cook fresh meat, dry wet clothes, cure the shivers, and keep everyone warm who huddled around its essence throughout the winter. There were rumours that it could do much more than this.
He remembered that the gods had called it "fire".

We have seen days at Kitty Hawk that would take the breath away. Days when the sun is warm on our faces and the breeze is gentle and strong and invites the world to come flying if it will only dare.

Just make one more tiny adjustment – one small change to a strut or a lever or the tip of a wing – and you will soar above the sand and the waves and the ignorance that has kept you earth-bound. You will look down on all you fly over – at the bench and the battery box and the launch-rail; at your footprints in the sand; at the ice-covered puddles and the wind-blown wrinkles; at the sheds of your camp and Big Kill Devil Hill; at the boats making wakes in the ocean; one more glance before they disappear – as if they are merely the toys of industrious ants.

The winds of Kitty Hawk will lift you up and carry you, on wings of your own devising, as far and as fast and as high as you have ever dreamed that a human can possibly go. Farther and faster and higher than any Greek god who ever had an unbelievable adventure in the pages of your sister-Katharine's books.

The one wing will rise higher and change the pressure above and below the wing. The other wing will move lower and change the pressure above and below the wing. The air moving over the wings will not be even and the wings will each react in a different way. One wing will rise and one wing will fall and the machine will move back to the level plane again.

This is the way that we will stabilize man in flight.

No, there is never any sacrifice, despite the sand that finds its way in through the cracks and the wind that whistles as it blows its way in past the door. Never any feeling that we don't want to be here.

The Arctic explorers often waited out a year, and sometimes two – trapped in their ships; facing scurvy and starvation; thoughts of mutiny and a yearning sickness for home – before the ice-pack would finally yield and let them through.

Octave Chanute left Kitty Hawk a month ago. After forty years of yearning for man to rise above the earth and fly, he complained that Kitty Hawk in December would be far too cold for him to stay.

He went home to where he could sit and read by the fire.

"There are certain ideas to which the Ancient Greeks clung with an eagle's talons," Katharine says, as she turns in the chair where she sits, preparing her lessons in the parlour, peering over-top of her glasses and tapping her book. "That flight is possible is one of those ancient ideas."

A twenty-seven mile an hour wind. A new and untried machine. A new system for warping the wing-tips, a new rear rudder. We have a machine that has never been flown before. The elevator is over-sensitive. We didn't have time to test it. We haven't even tried her as a glider. The ideal wind is eighteen to twenty miles per hour. Those winds out there are anything between twenty-five and thirty miles an hour. We are running out of days. The coffee pot and the newspaper. Drawing the bench up closer to the fire. Reading of our rivalry with Professor Langley. Sipping coffee and hoping that the wind will soon die down.

Chapter 2
Wilbur Wright 1

The Atlantic Ocean
May 26, 1908

Somewhere on the Atlantic Ocean. Suspended between America and France.

Lying my head back down on the pillow. Rocking back and forth. The pillow is soaked with my night-sweat. How does one sleep amid the swells? Troughs followed by hills of water; hills of water followed by troughs. Hour after hour, wave after wave, and so far not a wink of sleep. Time is passing. We first flew at Kitty Hawk almost five years ago. Staring up at the ceiling. I know the ceiling is there, but I cannot see it. My eyes are open, but the darkness is complete.

They were trapped inside the labyrinth. Icarus and his father, Daedalus. And what bothered Icarus most of all was that it was the labyrinth that his father had invented. It was Daedalus who had made it for King Minos when Icarus was just a boy. And now, due to a dispute between his father and the king, they were trapped within the walls of the labyrinth.

There is no difference between the night and the day. What pokes and prods me during the night, and what disturbs me during the day, is the nightmare nature of what my life has now become.

I am sure that for Orville it has become the same.

"Does the competition worry you, Mr. Wright?"

"Are you worried, Mr. Wright, about the flights that have been made successfully in France?"

"Do you think that your patent will hold up against the counter-claims?"

We have become public property. The public has bought stock in our imagination. They have attached themselves to our dreams. From now on, every gesture, every action, every thought, will be accompanied by a barrage of probing questions.

We are forced to separate – Orville and me. After ten years of talking, working, thinking and inventing as one person, we are being forced to work and think and demonstrate our flying machine as individuals. I must demonstrate in France and Orville in America at the same time.

It is the worst thing that could have happened to either of us. It is a nightmare.

I worry about Orville being alone in Washington. I am afraid that he will not tell me if he is unhappy with the situation at Fort Myer. I suspect he will be unhappy with the parade ground, but he will keep it to himself. I will write to Katharine about my concern. I will insist that she tell me what Orville is thinking.

Things have not gone very smoothly since 1903. The invention of the flying machine, and getting her into the air, has proven to be the easiest part, by far, of the enterprise.

Sitting on a deck chair in the sunshine. On the warmest side of the ship. Scanning a stack of newspapers. Looking for the latest news of the battle of the invention of the flying machines. The French are the most advanced, but Orville and I are far ahead of them. Surely there is nothing to be feared from the French.

"Well, I guess if we're ever going to get out of here, we'd better start quite soon," Daedalus said to his son, Icarus. "It is a matter of trial and error. Making a decision and hoping it works. Then, if it fails to be productive, we will have to retrace our steps and start all over again. The frustrating thing about a labyrinth is that while it is logic that is needed, it is guess-work that one is given as a guide. I have a feeling that we will be here for a very long time."

We have been faced with a conundrum: how to demonstrate our flying machine without giving away our secrets. How to secure a contact for our machine before the buyer is allowed to see our wares?

This is what we have insisted upon. No doubt, we have created a conundrum for potential customers as well.

"Why have you not flown your invention in public Mr. Wright?"
"Why the need for secrecy?"
"Is it because you cannot deliver on your claims?"

It had all seemed so easy, and yet it hadn't.

We seemed to have two ideas in our heads that day at Kitty Hawk. One of them was right and one was wrong.

One idea was the assumption that all would be easy, once we had flown. That we would perfect the Flyer and demonstrate it publicly, and be given credit for our work, and arrange to make our invention available to all the world.

Our other assumption was that we should be very careful – secretive and alert, cautious and mistrustful – proceeding carefully, as one would tread barefoot in a region of poisonous snakes, as we negotiate the long road ahead of us: the need to evolve a practical flying machine from the less-than-perfect machine that we had flown.

Both ideas were at full tide in our minds that day.

We should never have left the Flyer by herself.

The idle chatter of the passengers. "Are you taking a machine with you, Mr. Wright, or will you have one waiting for you there, when you get to France?" "Why is your brother not travelling with you?" "I had assumed that you and your brother were all but inseparable; I hadn't expected to see either one of you travelling alone."

The first day that we flew, in December 1903, we made the assumption that we would have lunch and then fly to Kitty Hawk, four miles away, to send a telegram, announcing our success, in the world's first heavier-than-air, controlled, human-piloted flying machine.
That assumption turned out to be a very good joke on us.
While we were chatting about our success, a gust of wind came along and rolled the Flyer over and over, splintering our machine and our complacency.
And that was the end of flying for that year.

The sea spreads out in front of the ploughing steamship. Nary a wrinkle on the surface for miles and miles ahead - not an identifiable landmark in sight. Not a seagull, not a tiny speck on the horizon. How is it that the captain is able to find his way?

In 1903, Octave Chanute was elated at our success.
His first note was a vessel which was filled with joy.
"I am immensely pleased by your success. Please advise me when I may be allowed to make the announcement public. I know that the world is waiting for just such an announcement. I have primed the scientific world for news of just such a breakthrough for over forty years, and the general public will certainly be thrilled, of that I can assure you."

Sitting on a deck-chair and shaking the wrinkles out of a newspaper. It is difficult to concentrate. The pages are constantly being ruffled by the breeze.
"Henri Farman has flown, in a Voisin-designed machine, at Issy-les-Moulineaux, for one minute and thirty-four seconds – a distance of almost three thousand, four hundred feet."

It is five years now since we flew at Kitty Hawk. In all that time, the other inventors have not come close to what we have done. Santos-Dumont, Farman, Blériot, The Voisin Brothers, Curtiss – not one of them has built a practical, heavier-than air, piloted, controlled flying machine.

How many invitations to shuffleboard can I refuse? How many books in the ship's library can I start and then not read? How many plans for the flying machine can I poke at with the pencil and then put aside? How many hours can it possibly be before we land in France?

If we demonstrate our flying machine in public, there are many who will copy what they see, ignore the patents, confuse the courts, and use our own ideas to compete with us.
We insist that we be given credit for our accomplishments. We have vowed to keep control of our ideas.

"Why have the Americans shown so little interest in your invention, Mr. Wright?"
"Why has the American Army been so reluctant to buy your machine?"
"It is possible that your machine will never fly?"

I wish that I was home.
At home, I would be sitting in the parlour, helping Father to go over his accounts. Searching for the out-of-logic number that will start the whole stack of numbers tumbling to the ground.
There is something in the numbers that does not seem right.

They were lost inside the labyrinth. Icarus and his father, Daedalus.
They were wandering for the second day and were getting nowhere. Perhaps they were close to the exit, but, if so, there was no way of knowing. Each time they failed, they started over again, retracing their steps from the very beginning. It was impossible to build on what they had done in the past.
The little nick in the leather of his left sandal threatened to drive Icarus mad. It seemed to be mocking him each time it appeared in the sand.

Sitting at the Captain's table. It seems that eventually every passenger will get to take a turn. Making small-talk as we eat. "Is this the iceberg season, Captain?" "Oh I hope not; it sounds so dangerous!" "Oh I'd love to see an iceberg!" "Is it not possible to sail quite close, Captain, and yet not come to any harm?"

Occasionally, Icarus and Daedalus would come across a basket of food. Icarus began to grow irritated with his father. Daedalus seemed to think that the highlight of the first day was finding two baskets of food. He was pleased to find a new one, instead of the empty shell of the one that they had devoured two hours before.
"We will never find our way out of here," sighed Daedalus, grunting heavily as he extracted a chicken leg from the basket. "I have done my work too well. I have designed a labyrinth from which no human can escape."

"Have you been following the news of the French attempts at flight, Mr. Wright?"
"Why do you not do your experiments in public as the French do, Mr. Wright?"
"Are you going to Europe to study the achievements of the French?"

Leaning on the railing as the ship ploughs on for France. Thinking what I must do when I arrive: find a suitable flying field; inspect the engines that we are having made; unpack the Flyer that Orville has sent; negotiate with businessmen; find a way to dodge the newsmen. Figure out a way to work in peace.

I wish I was at home.
At home, I would be listening to Katharine tell her stories of ancient Greeks and Renaissance wise-men. I could be sitting in the parlour, beside the crackling fire, with Orville and Katharine and Father, at this very moment.

Watching the crew perform a fire drill. Watching the crew climb into the lifeboat. Listening to the boatswain barking the orders. The ship is sinking fast. There is no time for idleness or confusion. The crew has manned their stations. Volunteer passengers are being loaded. A routine that has been designed to save their lives. Thank God that it is only a precautionary drill.

A stack of newspapers beside me as I sit on a deck-chair. The sun is pleasant, but the wind keeps threatening to snatch the news right out of my hands.
"Henri Farman has made a circle. In a flight of eighty-eight seconds, he has managed to make a turn. This is the first turn every made by a flying machine in France."

If we have been hurt at all by our competitors, it is because they have made the people with whom we negotiate suspect that flying is impractical. The lack of success, the minimal advances, the exaggerated claims and minuscule results of everyone who has experimented in public has placed our own claims in disrepute.
But now we feel that we are ready. Now we are ready to demonstrate publicly what the Flyer can do.

Watching the wake of the churning propellers. Watching the foam as it drifts away. How long will the mark remain in the water? How long will the track that we make on the ocean be there to indicate the path that we have made?

"Actually, we are not lost at all," said Daedalus, as Icarus grumbled about setting out on the third day of wandering inside the labyrinth.
"What do you mean, Father?" Icarus asked. He wondered how his father could speak with such unconcern. "I'd say that we look pretty lost to me. We have been wandering around for two days, tracing and retracing our steps, meeting our own footprints in the sand each time we come to believe that we are moving ahead."
"Don't forget that the palace was designed by me," Daedalus said. "One of my most delightful innovations, according to King Minos, was the idea that the palace should be perched above the labyrinth, so the king could watch his prisoners try fruitlessly to find their way back out of the maze. The second most delightful innovation – though really a minor one I assured him – was that he have a flag-pole on the turret, with a flag that would indicate the days when the king is in residence."
Icarus looked at his father in disbelief.
"I wanted the king to watch us fail to escape the maze."

In 1903, Octave Chanute was our biggest booster. He could hardly wait to spread the wonderful news.
"I am sorely tempted to make the announcement myself. I can barely restrain myself, but realize that it is only fitting that you, yourselves, should be allowed to make the first announcement of your achievement. I must warn you, though, that there might well be scepticism. No doubt, I shall be called upon to make a public pronouncement upon the event, in the wake of your credibility-challenging claim. To put my seal of approval, as it were, on your success."

My pillow is soaked with night-sweat.
Once again I have had a nightmare. About one of those ancient Greeks. One of the gods? Or maybe a mortal? I can't remember now. Perhaps the story of the labyrinth. The one about the people who are trapped inside. I will have to write to Katharine,

when I get to France, and ask her to tell me that story once again.

How could I dream when I have never closed my eyes?

I wish I were at home.

At home, Orville and I would be sitting on the trolley, on the way to Huffman Prairie, not saying a word to each other, but knowing that we are thinking that we are the only ones on the trolley who know that the world's first successful flying machine is waiting in a shed at the next stop on the line.

The process of selling the Wright Flyer will take much longer than we ever could have anticipated. I grow afraid that we will not be back in the bicycle shop for a long, long time.

I hope that Orville will tell me if the drill field at Fort Myer is not satisfactory, but I am afraid that he will keep it to himself.

I will write to Katharine and ask if Orville has written to her about the drill field. Perhaps he will tell Katharine what he refuses to share with me.

Neither Orville nor I should ever work alone. We never should have agreed to separate.

"Don't you think that the French are far ahead of everyone when it comes to flying?"

"Wouldn't any thinking person have to acknowledge that as a simple fact?"

"Is it not true, Mr. Wright, that even you would be forced to agree?"

"Today, King Minos has left the island, so we can leave at any time," Daedalus explained. "He will not be here to tell the guards that we have escaped. Really, my son, you underestimate me. Did you think that I would invent a labyrinth and not invent a way to ensure the inventor's escape? There is no conundrum that is greater than the human mind."

"But that is ingenious Father," Icarus sputtered. "I can admire what you have done. I am glad that we are not lost. But why, as we wandered around for two exhausting days – sore and angry and frustrated – did you not tell me?"

"Are you enjoying the ocean voyage, Mr. Wright?"

Lying my head back on the pillow and staring at the darkness of the ceiling. A few more hours until the morning. What time would it be back home? I sent a letter to Orville from New York. A crisis has arisen. He must act as soon as he can. I know that I should have taken care of it myself, before I left, but I was too busy with preparations for my voyage. Everything that I have done has been done in a rush. It can only be a few more hours until morning. I hope that things will begin to go well when I get to France.

Chapter 3
Orville Wright 1

On the Train
May 23, 1908

Somewhere in the darkness, on a train.
Lying on my back. Swaying back and forth. I feel as if I am on rollers. The light strikes in slashes through the slats of the blind. The sleeper of a railroad car. Suspended between Washington D.C. and Dayton, Ohio. Time is pressing. We flew at Kitty Hawk over four years ago.

Phaeton was having problems at his school. Another boy laughed at him when Phaeton told him who he was.
"The son of Apollo?" the other boy sneered. "Don't be ridiculous. I don't see any resemblance. How could a person like you be the son of such a god?"

A letter from Wilbur, sent before he sailed from New York.
"I saw an article in the newspaper about the flying machine that Glenn Curtiss is building. It infringes our patent for the warping of the wings. I think that a statement which describes our original features should be imprinted very soon on the public mind. It is only our competitors who read the news from the patent office. We need the public on our side. Maybe you could try the Century magazine."

Wilbur and I are separated. For the first time in our lives, we are not sleeping in the same building. For the first time in ten years, we are not eating, talking, arguing and thinking together, on a moment-by-moment basis, every day.
It was a business decision. If Wilbur and I are going to keep our secrets until the moment when our prospective customers are ready to sign on the dotted line, then we must demonstrate the Wright Flyer to the U.S. Army and the conglomerate in France at the same time.
If we were to do our demonstrations here – or there – and not obtain a contract, we would be giving our secrets free to every unscrupulous inventor in the world.

The positions in the stalemate were very clear.

The Army would not buy our flying machine until we had provided a demonstration; we would not demonstrate our flying machine until the Army had agreed to buy. Why should we show our secrets to everyone who is interested in dodging the patents and stealing our ideas?

The Army is very stubborn, but so are we. It took a long time, and many talks, to break the stalemate.

Perhaps the impending sale to the French has made them budge.

"Why has the Army demanded a trial of your invention, Mr. Wright?"
"Does this mean that there is little faith in your machine?"
"Why do you say that you must practice before you can fly?"

We have become a staple of the news. If we move or if we don't, if we act or if we refuse, if we fly or remain on the ground, it will be reported. Every momentary nod, every doubt as to what to do next, every weary resignation, will be probed with the sharp point of another incisive question.

I worry about Wilbur being alone in France.

Wilbur does not speak French, beyond a smattering. I fear that Wilbur is too impatient to always say 's'il vous plaît' when he wants something done.

I should have gone to France while he stayed here.

We have not won the negotiations, but we have not lost.

We have finally come to an agreement with the United States Army. We have an agreement for the Army to buy, in principle; the Army has an agreement for us to demonstrate, with certain restrictions.

A limited number of sworn and trusted observers; no photographs or note-making on the site; perhaps we can protect our ideas while hawking them on the street corners of America and Europe.

The possibility of failure is the cause for sleepless nights.

The situation is a nightmare. I find I cannot sleep. I must have tossed and turned all night. The pillow is soaking wet and my head is aching. How close am I to home? I wonder what time it is. Spreading the slats of the blind. The train rolls through the landscape, towards Dayton, in the dark of the night.

I miss the family back at home.

Home is the ice-cream parlour around the corner from the bicycle shop on West Third Street.

It was Father who came home with the news that the new ice-cream parlour was open. First he took Wilbur, and then he took me, and then he took Lorin, and then Netta and the children.

It was only when we talked together that we realized that Father must be the new ice-cream parlour's most frequent customer.

Ever since 1906, we have had a legal patent on our work.

Since 1906, anyone can send for a copy of the patents and make flying machines that are virtually copies of our machine. Our only means of protection are the good will of the other inventors and the courts. In which of these would it be wise to place our faith?

We have finally come to an agreement with the United States Army.

I must fly a heavier-than-air flying machine, with a passenger, a distance of one hundred and twenty-five miles, at a speed of forty miles per hour. I must remain aloft for one hour minimum and land without damage. The flying machine must be capable of dismounting and loading on an Army wagon for transportation. The flying machine must permit an intelligent man to become proficient in its use within a reasonable length of time.

The Wright Flyer is more than capable. The capabilities of the Wright Flyer are not in doubt.

"But I am the son of a god," Phaeton cried. "Apollo is my father. When I visit him, on the weekends, he always lets me drive the Chariot of the Sun."

"Now I know you're telling lies," the other boy replied. "My father says that no one but Apollo will ever be allowed to drive the Chariot of the Sun. Next time you lie, you'd better mention some other god."

Phaeton turned around and ran fast until he reached his home.

Rolling through the landscape in the darkness of the night. On my way home to Dayton, to prepare a flying machine to demonstrate to the U.S. Army. Without Wilbur, whom I have worked with on a daily basis for the last ten years. I must also send a flying machine to France.

"Why is your brother demonstrating the air machine in a foreign country, Mr. Wright?"

"Why would you want to place your machine in foreign hands?"

"Are you and your brother not patriotic, Mr. Wright?"

Why were we so complacent after the success of getting the Flyer off the ground?

We have seldom been so careless. We gave ourselves a few tiny moments to relax, and to enjoy our success – after years of sand and wind and setbacks; but also of gains and advances and successes. To stand beside the Wright Flyer, the first heavier-than-air machine to ever be successful at controlled, sustained, powered human-carrying flight.

We never should have relaxed our guard that way.

I awake from a disturbing dream. What time is it, I wonder? Where have I put my watch? How many more hours until we reach Dayton? Who will meet me at the station? I wonder if Katharine and Father are expecting me. I can't remember if I told them when I would arrive.

We stood beside the Flyer – complacency in our minds – and discussed the great achievement that we had made. We would try her one more time. A longer flight this time. How about a flight that will take us all the way to Kitty Hawk, four miles over the sand? Why not enjoy the first flush of powered human flight? We could fly to the telegraph office and trumpet our success.

As we gloated at our triumph over the mighty winds, a little puff of air came along and destroyed our illusions.

Clymene was out in the garden, with a basket and some scissors and a large straw hat to shield her from the sun. She was gathering flowers for the table. Bluebells, tulips, chrysanthemums and a single blue rose. She would gather flowers in the garden every day.

"Mother", Phaeton sniffled. "A boy at school has laughed at me. I told him who my father was. He said my father could never be the god of the sun."

Sitting in the club-car and fishing in my bag for a number of items that I feel that I should read.

A mention, in *L'Aéronaute*, of Octave Chanute.

"Unlike some others who are involved in the field of aeronautics, Monsieur Chanute believes in the sharing of ideas in a common cause. The distinguished gentleman also believes, as he ages, that it is imperative that he train young, intelligent and daring pupils who will be able to carry his flying ideas to their greatest heights. Among these pupils, he considers the most principal to be the Brothers Wright."

The Flyer was caught by the breeze. As we were standing and talking about how to word the message of our success, the Flyer tumbled over and over, just out of our reach, with snapping wires and splintering struts, and settled down as a broken heap in the Kitty Hawk sand.

So what if you have some success? So what if you reach the skies? So what if you create a new era in the history of mankind? A gentle breeze will take your pride and dump it in the sand.

No more flying for the season of 1903.

Lying on the bunk and looking at the lights on the ceiling. Swaying with the swaying of the train. What was it that Wilbur wrote in his last letter? He mailed it from New York before embarking for France. Why can't I remember the things that I need to know?

I miss the family back at home.

Home is Katharine baking pies on a Saturday, and putting them on the windowsill to cool. And making tarts with the left-over cherries, and peaches and apples, so Wilbur and I don't have to wait to get a taste until supper-time.

Blueberry pie is the greatest invention in the history of mankind.

Walking up the sidewalk, on the way home from the bicycle shop, makes us realize that 7 Hawthorne Street, Dayton Ohio, is the culinary centre of the world.

"Is it true, Mr. Wright, that your flying machine was built in a bicycle shop?"

"How could you match the resources that Professor Langley was able to command?"

"What can you do that Professor Langley couldn't manage to do?"

Katharine will surely know. She will know what Wilbur wrote. Something about the machine that I should look after. I will ask her when I see her, but it will be hours before the train arrives in Dayton. Why does everything slip away while I am asleep?

"Well, the boy was wrong, but so were you," Clymene said to Phaeton. She put the single blue rose and the scissors into her basket. "I knew this day would happen eventually. I dreaded that it would come. That is why I made you promise never to tell anyone that you knew who your father was. You are growing up faster than I realize. I think it is time for you to go and ask your father to acknowledge you. When he does, you have a right to ask for a wish. He is pledged to give you anything under the sun."

I will have to work alone when I get back home. I have many things to do. I must build an entirely new version of the Flyer. I must prepare myself to fly the Army trials. There are machines that I must prepare for shipment to France. And there was something else that Wilbur insisted that I must do. My trip to Washington was disappointing. The field is smaller than any field where we have flown before.

"How do you explain the absence of your mentor, Mr. Chanute?"
"Why would you and your brother not be demonstrating the air machine together, Mr. Wright?"
"Is there truth to any of the rumours that the two of you are estranged?"

Sitting in the club-car and reading in the dusk. The reading-lantern glows and people nod as they gradually make their peace with the evening news. Slowly, the darkness falls across the land.
An article, in *L'Aéronaute*, on Octave Chanute.
"For several years, Mr. Chanute has been applying himself with indefatigable earnestness to the difficult problem of aerial navigation by heavier-than-air means. He has built innumerable gliders, each one making a slight improvement over the former. He has experimented with tireless patience and precision of method and his advances had made him a veritable celebrity among aviators. Monsieur Chanute was kind enough to outline the principle behind the idea of wing-warping."

It rained almost every day when I was in Washington. I am worried about the parade-ground where I will fly. The landing surface is very rough. We have always been very careful in choosing our flying fields. A five-mile circuit, over rough terrain, to Alexandria and back, with very few places that are fit for me to land. No more of Kitty Hawk's soft-landing sand. The Army has no idea of what kind of conditions a flying machine needs.

I miss the family back at home.
Home is the family – Father, Wilbur, Katharine and I – gathered in the parlour, on a cold winter evening, with the crackling of the fire and the snow swirling around under the eves and tapping against the window-pane, while we say our evening prayers.
There is no warmth – physical or spiritual – anywhere in the world like there is at home.

How is it possible to go without sleeping and still have nightmares? This is a phenomenon that I have noticed before. The number of times I have searched for my watch, as the train sways and sashays its way around the curves, means that I have had almost no sleep at all. And yet I am sure that I have dreamed for what must have been many hours. I seem to remember a dream about a Greek god. I must ask Katharine about those old stories when I get back home.

Sitting in the club-car and resting my eyes. Taking a letter out and reading it once again.

A reply from Glenn Curtiss.

"I wish to reassure you, Mr. Wright, beyond the shadow of a doubt, that I have no intention of entering the exhibition business with the flying machine that I have designed. The newspapers were erroneous in that assumption. My intentions are experimental only. As to the question of patent infringement, I have directed the matter to the attention of the secretary of our association."

Phaeton trudged up the steps of the palace of the sun god. The steps were steep and lined with sentries, and every one of them bowed to the boy. They had heard that he was the son of the god, Apollo.

The golden doors were open, and Phaeton walked inside. His footsteps echoed loudly as he entered the room. He squinted at the blinding light that struck his eyes.

Through the slits, he could see a great god at the far, far end of the golden throne-room.

"How can you justify, Mr. Wright, the expense of public money?"
"Hasn't the Langley fiasco been public expense enough?"
"Does the Army believe that your contraption will leave the ground?"

I worry about Wilbur being alone.

He does not speak the language where he has gone. Our means of communicating without words will not work very well for Wilbur while he is in France. The two of us can work for many hours and never speak, but with others, I find I must be explaining myself every moment of the day.

How is Wilbur going to explain himself in French?

Neither Wilbur nor I should ever work alone. We never should have agreed to separate.

Was it a god or was it a mortal? Katharine would know for sure. I will ask her just as soon as I see her again. There was the god and there was the son. There was disagreement between them. That is about all I can remember from my dream. There was something about the sky. And something about some horses. And something about a promise that was made without thought. Why is it that dreams slip away in the dark of the night?

"Please be so kind as to approach the throne," a booming voice called out to Phaeton. The voice seemed to be bounding off the walls. "I have an inkling who you are. But I would rather hear from you just what you are doing here."

A group of people chuckled from far away.

Phaeton stood and waited for a little while. The light from the throne was blinding. He couldn't clear his eyes well enough to see.

"What is the reason you are here?" the voice from the end of the room boomed out. "Don't be shy, my little man. Come and tell me who you are. I am wondering how

I can be of any help."

Again, there was a muffled chuckle from the end of the room.

It is hard to trust Glenn Curtiss. The description in the article of the way in which he intends to control the flying machine is a direct infringement of the special features of our patent for the Flyer. Nevertheless, in his letter, he complains of a lack of control in his design. I couldn't resist suggesting that this was due to the improper arching of the wing-surfaces. Perhaps I should be less generous with my advice.

"Why don't you try your hand at alchemy, Mr. Wright?"

I spread my fingers and open the blinds. I am somewhere in Ohio. I am somewhere in the morning. Somewhere ahead there is Dayton, and I will soon be home. What was it that Wilbur wanted me to do? I must ask Catherine about Wilbur's letter when I get back home.

Chapter 4
The Wright Brothers 2

Kitty Hawk, North Carolina
December 17, 1903

A cold day at Kitty Hawk.
Ten o'clock in the morning. Now or never. Eighty-four days in camp. Running low in food. Cold and getting colder. Winter coming on. And we are confident that the machine will work if the wind will cooperate. Besides, we have told ourselves we are going to be home for Christmas. The wind is blowing fiercely. Somehow, we'll manage the wind. Decision time at last. We are thinking exactly the same. A nod is as good as a word. Yes, today will be the day that we will fly.

Prometheus couldn't sleep. All night, he took turns climbing the tree and then, an hour or so later, climbing back down again.

From the branch, he could see the glow on Mount Olympus. He had been there and he kept thinking of what it would be to have the power that was vested in the gods.

When he was down on the ground, he couldn't see the glow. His eyes peered out at the darkness, but he couldn't see. Once in a while he would shiver. His skin would pucker up and he would rub his arms and legs to restore the warmth.

He doubted that there would be shivering among the gods.

The problem, as we have defined it, is one of lift. How is man to raise himself up off the ground and fly through the air like a bird? The problem is that man is not a bird. He does not have the power to lift himself aloft and fly through the air. The question is how to raise and sustain a man's weight above the ground? What shape of wing will carry him through the air?

Data, facts, numbers, definitions. The water we swim in; the air we breathe. To glide higher, faster longer than man has every glided before. To encounter problems that no one has ever encountered before.

Span-to-cord ratio - centre of pressure - leading edge - degree of camber - one-

in-eight - one-in-twenty-four - lift-drag ratio - angle of incidence - resistance of drag-curved airfoils.

Kitty Hawk is cold in mid-December. We came here to catch the winds. We came here to fly our kites, and to test our gliders, in winds that are ideal to give us lift. In sands that are ideal to cushion our landings.

Kitty Hawk is wonderful in the autumn with the sun rising over the ocean and the gulls drifting over the waves, but we never planned to be at Kitty Hawk as late as December.

We have already flipped a coin. The Flyer is only made to carry one. We have promised Father that we will never fly together. That is as it should be. It is safer if only one of us takes to the air. We think of ourselves as "we". Physically, we are apart; mentally, we are together. All of our work has been as one. The turning of every nut and the tightening of every wire is being done by the two of us. The inventor of the flying machine, and the pilot of every flight, no matter who is on the ground or in the air, is the Wright Brothers.

Leonardo's bag cut into his shoulder. The notebook was heavy and bulky. Someday, he would sort the pages out. Too much to carry without any sorting for weeks at a time. The sun was gradually moving over the hills.

Beauty, strength and what? Something else. Something that mankind doesn't possess. At least not now. The humblest bird can soar without effort. Can leap off a cliff or step off a tree and fly through the air. Looking down on we superior beings, as we plod along on the ground, wondering why we fight our way through the thickets when we could be soaring on the currents of the air just as they do.

What is the knowledge that makes the birds take so easily to flight?

How to attach an apparatus to the weight of man that will be such that the combined weight of the man and machine will be overcome by the lifting power of the apparatus? How to ensure that the wind on the wings that will be added to the man will lift him and carry him safely through the air?

Small aspect ratio - thin bird-wing profiles - biplane performance - thick leading edges - Langley's model - arc - strap iron - 24" x 24" x 8" - recheck vane - fan.

Shoulder against the door. Pushing through the wind. Tacking the flag up on the side of the shed. To summon the members of the Life Saving Station at Kill Devil Hills. Red for flying. Bet they won't believe we're going to fly. We've never joked with the flag before, but today they'll wonder.

What size shall these wings be? How long? How wide? How thick? What materials and fabric shall these wings be made of? What shape shall these wings have? Square or round? Flat or curved? All of these questions must be answered before anyone will ever be able to fly.

Steady airflow - six feet long - sixteen inches square - pane of glass - fan - leading edges - trailing edges - current of wind - wind straightener - resistance plane.

Kitty Hawk is cold and drizzling rain on the work-inside days, and bitter winds and ice on the puddles on the work-outside days. Kitty Hawk in mid-December is a great provoker of thoughts of what it would be like to be at home.

Home is the four of us, sitting in the parlour on winter evenings and reading with the fire dancing warmly in the fireplace. Katharine pouring over her lesson plans on the daily jousting that went on between the ancient Greek gods and the human heroes. Father, pouring over his church accounts, trying to find the flaw in the ledger, the unaccounted-for entry which will bring down a financial house of illicit cards. And we, with our aeronautical papers, pouring over everything that we can find that has been published so far, scrutinizing every theory and every design and every number that has been recorded on the topic. Trying to solve the riddle of human flight.

Warming the hands against the fire. A pause for a cup of coffee and another look at the newspaper. Strange how the sand is so adept at finding its way between the pages. A good shake clears the pages before we read.
"Yes, of course I am using public money," Professor Langley is admitting to the newspapers. "Yes, the Army has granted me a stipend of fifty thousand dollars, in order to continue to conduct my experiments in human flight. The Smithsonian Institution has been generous as well. No, the threat of war is no longer imminent. Yes, the crisis in Cuba has now receded. But for future military conflict, it is logical to say that control of the air will be imperative to ensure success. This has always been the case. This has been acknowledged since Leonardo's time."

It is the only decision we could possibly make, with Professor Langley pressing on our heels. Somehow, if the information in the newspapers can be believed, we know he can't possibly fly. Not with the reported weight and size and strength of his ungainly machine, and the reported design that the professor had chosen for the wings. Still, not everything printed in the newspapers can be believed. We can't take the chance. It is mid-December and growing colder. We have the rest of the winter and then the summer bicycle season in the shop ahead of us. We must fly now or not be able to attempt to fly for almost a year. Despite the wind, we feel we have no choice. It is just possible that Professor Langley's machine will be able to fly.

Thousands of years have passed with very meagre knowledge. Man has studied birds in flight for thousands of years. Very little has been added to our knowledge of the science of flight in all that time. Man has glided as a bird, but not very far. Man has measured his time in the air, so far, in seconds.

Wind velocity - atmospheric conditions - lift balance - pressure on a square plate - variations in current - resistance strip - aerofoil- parallel arms - connecting links - negative angle.

A pile of books on the table in the parlour. A fire in the fireplace. Warmth on winter nights. Everything that we can possibly find to read on the question of human flight.
Aerial Navigation, Animal Mechanism, Aeronautical Annual, A Text-Book of Applied Mechanics, Animal Locomotion: Or Walking Swimming and Flying with a Dis-

sertation on Aeronautics, Progress in Flying Machines, Experiments in Aerodynamics, The Aeronautical Annual, Empire of the Air, The Problem of Flying and Practical Experiments in Soaring, Story of Experiments in Mechanical Flight, On Soaring Flight.

Leonardo paused and caught his breath. The path was smooth, but the climb was very steep. Many had been here before and the way was not so difficult, but he kept up a steady pace, because he planned to go as high as he could possibly go. Far above him, he could see the peak where he wanted to be.

The birds have beauty, strength and knowledge of how to fly. The drawings are designed to unite the attributes of the flying-bird and the flightless-man. The drawings are designed to explore how a man could be fitted with wings that will allow him to leave the earth behind and soar.

A mythological creature? One certainly hates to think so. This is surely the age of man, not of the gods. It is a matter of acquiring the knowledge of the mechanical demands of flight. A matter of understanding the currents of the air and how they interact with the movement of the wings. It was a matter of designing the best combination of weight and strength and power.

Surely the age is beckoning man to learn to fly.

"Right over there would be perfect for the track." About thirty yards west of the sheds. About three hundred yards north of Big Kill Devil Hill. "Perfectly level for a distance of a quarter of a mile." Then lugging the pieces of launch-rail. Fifteen-foot sections. Two-by-fours with a metal strip along the top. "The Junction Railroad." From south to north to catch the lift of the wind. "The water has levelled the sand nearly flat, so there won't be much need of preparation for laying the track."

Octave Chanute was very gracious. As we sat around the campfire, at Kitty Hawk, in the shadow of Big Kill Devil Hill, he reminded us of how it was in the early days.

"When you wrote to me," he said, "I had no hesitation in doing what I always do with everyone who writes to me for guidance. I wrote back to you and encouraged you, and sent you everything that I had that I thought would help you. I asked you about your work, and how you felt it might contribute to the ages-old desire for human flight. I encouraged you, as I have encouraged every young enthusiast who has followed after me. I have always seen your quest as complementary to my own."

The question concerns the configuration of the wings. The Chanute-Herring glider gives us help. The Pratt Truss has been used on bridges: two surfaces, bound together with vertical posts and cross-bracing for the optimum combination of maximum strength with minimum weight. This is an idea that we can learn from. We will have two wings bound together in the Pratt Truss configuration, as developed by Octave Chanute.

Camber variations - large aspect ratio - triplane performance - varying gaps - plin's curve - 16" x 16" - vane-type balance - bicycle-wheel testing - grinderhead - tapered tips.

A pile of books on the table in the parlour. All of the authors that we are aware of who have tackled the age-old question of human flight.

Sir George Cayley, Etienne Jules Marey, James Means, Andrew Jamieson, J. Bell Pettigrew, Octave Chanute, Samuel P. Langley, Louis-Pierre Mouillard, E. C. Huffaker, Otto Lilienthal and Henry S. Pilcher.

This slight depression was covered by water a few days ago. Smoothing the sand with the shovel, here and there. "That's perfect." Setting the sections down and pinning each one down on the sand. Bitter blasts from off the beach. The wind goes through the coat and tickles the marrow. Hustling back to the shed to warm the hands.

Prometheus sat in the dark. He leaned his back against the tree and rubbed his arms and legs to restore the warmth. Occasionally, a wolf would howl in the distance.

How could heat be locked in wood? What was fire that it would release this kind of energy? When you bring two things together you discover a third.

What kind of creature is a man, he wondered. Is he made to remain earthbound, forever, climbing up each mountain and picking his way down – sliding in the shale; uncertain footstep by uncertain footstep – into each valley? Fighting his way through the thickets and brambles and the mud? Or is man a creature who has been made with the ability to soar?

Surely fire will make the difference. Surely fire will unlock the possibilities that are hidden in all things.

Cold and frost and sand. Hang the wet gloves near the stove and look for the newspaper.

Professor Langley, once again, explains his mission.

"Our design workshop," Professor Langley tells the reporters, "has brought together all of the knowledge and expertise that exists in the present state of the art of human flight. No, the money is not being wasted, not at all. The engine that we have devised is of gasoline power. The machine is double-winged and is equipped with an open car which will contain a human operator. Yes, the launch will take place on the Potomac River, forty miles downstream from the city of Washington, from the roof of a houseboat which has been anchored in mid-stream. Yes the wings of the dragonfly are the inspiration for the design."

The question deals with the curvature of the wings. There is no science that can tell us how to do this. For this, we must figure things out for ourselves. Birds have flown for thousands of miles and for many thousand years with curves in their wings. Man has flown successfully for seconds by using wings with a curve, but what kind of curve would support a man for hours?

Narrow vertical surfaces - constant in direction - aspect ratios - spans - cambers - flat planes - curved planes - tailing edges - square wing-tips - rounded wing-tips.

Der Vogelflug als Grundlage der Fliegekunst, by Otto Lilienthal. Sent to us, very generously, by Octave Chanute. German text and illustrations. A mouthful to pronounce and seemingly-impossible to read. The illustrations show a man who has attached wings to his arms and is jumping from a hill near Berlin.

Where there is a will, there is a way: late nights spent by the gas lamp with a German-English dictionary.

Laying the rest of the track. About 100 feet away from the shed. West side. Nice and level. Pointing due north. "It's working out just fine." "The starting end is a few inches lower than the launching end." One good thing about the wind. No need to launch her from a slope. If we want to call it flying, we will have to launch from the flat. We can't be doing our launching from the hill. Gravity must be ruled out as a factor. There must be no question that our machine is self-propelled. Cold. Returning to the shed to warm our hands.

We believe that there is nothing that a bird can do that a man can't do as well. If we can learn more about the curve of the wings, we too can fly for hours. But what curve should the air-foil be?

There are secrets in the winds. There are strange things that happen at certain heights and certain movements and certain speeds. The danger is that in creating a flying machine, a man might be designing a machine that will inevitably lead to his death.

A grim thought perhaps, but wasn't Dr. Guillotine the eventual victim of his own ingenuity?

Otto Lilienthal advanced the cause of human flight, but Otto Lilienthal's glider was the technical achievement that took his life. What was the cause of the sudden pitch forward and the fatal crash?

Bird-wing shapes- square shapes - oblong shapes - elliptical shapes - monoplanes - bi-planes - multi-wing planes - two hundred different configurations - wing curves - wing cambers.

Otto Lilienthal flew gliders. He made over two thousand glides. He established the supremacy of arched wings in preference to flat wings. He measured success in seconds. By throwing himself from a hill, he managed to fly for a total of five hours in the span of five years, making adjustments year-by-year in his design. Finally, he died, when his glider stalled, and he plunged straight down to the ground. A broken back and death within a day.

Otto Lilienthal flew gliders for seconds at a time, but we want a machine in which a man can fly for hours.

What should the curvature be for the air-foil? A camber of 1-in-12? Or 1-in-22? Or maybe somewhere in all the choices in between? A perfect arc? A curve in front? Or further back? Which curve for the wing is best?

So many kinds of birds, and all of them flying, so easily, every day. The winds attack them from all sides and they maintain their equilibrium by subtle moves. But the birds move so quickly that one cannot see the constantly-changing shape of their wings. Human problems need human solutions. We are into an area where watching the birds no longer offers help.

Parabolic curves - thick bird-wing profiles - high aspect ratio - tapering tips - varying cambers - Lilienthal's test surface - a second wind tunnel - seven-eighths inches in thickness - wallpaper scraps - wind-tunnel straightener.

Henry S. Pilcher was a pioneer of human flight. He would strap wings to himself and attempt to fly. He died in an experimental glider of the Lilienthal type. It was larger and heavier than any glider that Otto Lilienthal ever flew. He was giving a demonstration at Market Harborough when a gust of wind caught his wing and he plummeted to earth.

It is important to always move in advance of all previous knowledge. Often, the price of this advance is to fall from the sky. Which ideas to accept and which ideas to discard?

What dangers lurk in previous advances that we must identify and eliminate?

Body stiff and fingers numb from the damp and the cold. The rigging of the stove in the shed was a good idea. And one long overdue. Not much good out here, though, for the laying of the track. Hard to work with gloves on. Rubbing the hands very vigorously to restore the circulation of the blood. Someday, maybe, someone will invent a machine that will heat the whole outdoors. Too late for us if we freeze to death today.

After waiting forty years, with the patience of a mid-wife, why did Octave Chanute insist that it was far too cold for him to stay and be a witness to the first powered flight of humankind?

Leonardo gritted his teeth. The bag bit into his shoulder and his hip was aching. He had found a stick along the trail which had helped to ease the burden and take some of the weight. The hills of Florence increase in height in proportion to age.

The trail was narrower here, and less-well cleared. His sandals were good, but the sharper stones insisted on making their presence felt. If he kept up a steady pace, he would surely arrive where he wanted to be before noon.

Does bread weigh less in the stomach than when carried in a bag which is supported by an aching shoulder and an aging hip?

What shape to make the wings? The building of a wind tunnel. The controlling of the winds inside a box. Countless hours cutting out miniature wings. Two hundred shapes and thicknesses. Cutting and shaping the sets of model wings and placing them in the wind tunnel.

Measuring the lift of each model wing. Measuring the drag of each model wing. Measuring the performances of the air-foils over a series of angles of attack. Recording the statistics. Recording numbers that can be inserted into equations.

Dihedral wings - anhedral wings - aspect ratio designs - centre of pressure - centre of gravity - the balancing of the two - pitch control - surface area - downward pressure - reversal of movement of the centre of pressure - the centre of pressure moves with the centre of attack.

Then the truck. The yoke and the under-carriage. Fit the bicycle-hub rollers on the track. Then the skids will sit snugly on the truck. The bench we'll need as a wing-rest, to keep her level. The c-clamp to hold her down. The coil box, the connecting cables. The shovel. The can of nails and tacks and the hammer. We've seldom had a flight without needing repairs. Breaking the ice in the smaller puddles each time we move.

Prometheus stood up. The sun was coming up over the mountains. The rays were spreading across the hills. He stood up beside the tree and looked around him.

He had made a decision while crouching for hours in the dark.

He had no need to climb the tree. He knew where Olympus was, though he couldn't see it. If he started now, he should reach it about mid-day. He would be tired and he would ache but he would be there. He had thrashed his way through the underbrush and slid backwards on the shale when he had climbed Olympus before. The path would soon run out, but he would find his way. Just keep moving towards the sky, he told himself.

And this time, it will be different. This time, you will not talk to Zeus. This time, you are not asking Zeus for permission to realize your dreams.

Tomorrow, you will be the possessor of fire.

Octave Chanute was very cold. It was November at Kitty Hawk and he huddled as close as he could to the fire. He had to be warned two or three times that he was in danger of getting burned.

"I see everyone who is involved in the pursuit of human flight as a partner," he said. "That is you and that is I and that is Professor Langley. I believe that everyone should be as generous with their advances as I have always been with the theories and the knowledge that I have possessed. It might well be that yourselves, or Professor Langley – or others, perhaps very far in the future – might be the first to fly. The important thing is that when success is finally achieved, all will have contributed unselfishly for the benefit of all."

The men from the Kill Devil Hills Life Saving Station. Hunched down inside their collars. Bundled up warm against the wind. John T. Daniels and Will Dough and Adam Etheridge. Another man as well. "W. C. Brinkley is the name. The boys invited me along. I was looking at the timbers of a wreck. Lumber dealer from over Manteo way." Rubbing the hands together. A cloud of breath in the air. "Glad to have you." "Hope to show you something interesting today." Young Johnny Moore, from Nags Head, too. "Staying over at the station are you, Johnny?" "Glad you came along." That makes it five. Just about right. Important to have a group of witnesses along. "A flying machine, you say?" "Here, let us give you a hand to get her ready."

Huddling close to the carbide-can stove. Woodpile as close companion. Rugs on the wall to deflect the draft that sifts in through the cracks. Shaking the sand out of the newspapers and checking the latest news.

"The pilot of the craft," Professor Langley tells his readers, "will be Charles M. Manley. He is eminently qualified to be the controller of this machine. Yes, I realize that some have been sceptical. Perhaps these sceptics don't read the newspapers, or they would be more aware of the progress that mankind has seen. Don't forget, sir, that it was reported in your very own newspaper that a model of this very construction has flown. No, no human was on board that missile, I grant you that one point, but I see no difference between a model and a machine which is carrying a man. Fifty-two horsepower should be plenty of power to launch this young man skyward. Very soon, Mr. Manley is going to be famous. He will be the first human being to make a sustained flight in a self-propelled flying machine."

Why have these men died?

The air is unforgiving. There is no bouncing back from a mistake when you are fifty feet high in the air. There is no knowledge that you can draw on when you are the first human being to have ever soared so high.

The air plays strange tricks. There are as many eddies, backwaters and cross-currents in the air as in the turbulence of the rivers. Our reading has taught us some lessons. We have decided that these men died because of their failure to maintain equilibrium in the air. The failure was in the design. As soon as they were buffeted, they were lost.

The path to the future is strewn with the bodies of those who have died while in the pursuit of the elusive dream of human flight. The trick, as we have realized very early in our reading, is to design an experimental flying machine that will allow the inventor-operator to stay alive.

In this, perhaps, we can make ourselves unique.

How to free mankind to fly? Lift and drag and velocity. Values, variables, constants. Developing a table of lift coefficients. Otto Lilienthal's numbers are unreliable. We must go back to where he started and begin again.

Pushing past the point where the others have all gone wrong. Experimenting with a wind tunnel to find the ideal shape and size for human wings. What we know will eventually lift us into the air.

"Pegasus," Katharine says, "is a horse with wings." She is peering over her glasses as she works on her lessons in the parlour. We are momentarily exhausted in our endless discussions of the probable mechanics of human flight. "He prances along the ridge at the top of the hill. His coat is white and so is the spread of his wings. It is morning, and he reflects the light of the sun."

Carrying the parts of the Flyer over to the launching site. Putting her together. Main frame, tail frame, front rudder frame and surfaces. "She's a pretty heavy wind." "Surprised you picked today to try to fly." "Bob Wescott is going to watch her though the spyglass." "It was his turn to stay behind and make the lunch." "Where's Bill Tate and Alpheus Drinkwater?" "Drinkwater had something more important to do, but I don't know why Bill Tate hasn't come along."

Chapter 5
Wilbur Wright 2

Le Mans, France
July 4, 1908

A July day in France.
July 4th. A very special day at home, but just another day here, in France. Working hard on the Wright Flyer. Getting her ready to show the French what she can do. On July 14th, my host, Monsieur Bollée tells me, I will be invited to take the day off to help to celebrate the fall of the Bastille. At the risk of giving offence, I thanked him and said that I will stay right here and work alone.

Icarus reached down and grasped his father's wrist. Daedalus seized Icarus's wrist in turn. It gave them a double bond. Icarus grunted as he helped to pull his father's weight up onto the top of the promontory.

Icarus marvelled at his father's ingenuity. It was a relief to have escaped the bounds of the labyrinth so easily.

They looked out over the end of the island that they could see. They could not see the labyrinth from here, nor the palace of King Minos, but they could see enough to know what they must do.

There is no difference between the night and the day. What pokes and prods me during the night, and what disturbs me during the day, is the nightmare nature of what my life has now become.

I am sure that for Orville it has become the same.

Standing in front of the Wright Flyer. The motor revving up to optimum speed. The motor getting hot. The water boiling. Standing in front of the motor and taking the speed.

There are darker days ahead.
I have been greeted, here in France, as a disciple of Octave Chanute. When I arrived, I found that Octave Chanute had given talks in which he explained our ideas in detail. Now I am told that if an idea has been made public knowledge, it is public

property. Thanks to Octave Chanute, we have very little protection for our patents here in France.

Our only protection is in our precision; the hidden dimensions within the idea; what can't be estimated from a photograph or deduced from watching the machine as it moves through the air.

Our ideas are now on display in the store-front windows of the world. We have spent hundreds of hours developing nuances that a thief can smash and grab.

We must sell our ideas before others have plundered our dream.

I worry about Orville being alone in Washington. He has many things to contend with: the military, the crowds and the newspapermen. I am afraid that he will be sidetracked by their demands. Each one absorbs time and attention. It was a mistake to agree to come here. Perhaps I should postpone the trials in France and go home and help.

"We will go down to that cove," said Daedalus, "and there we will build a raft, and we will sail north until we reach some hospitable land."

They shuffled a little bit more. There was barely enough room for two to stand on the precipice. Daedalus looked up and watched a golden eagle, which was circling lazily, and pointed it out to Icarus.

"Waiting, perhaps, for we humans to leave his perch."

Meetings, meetings, meetings.

I tear myself away from preparations for my flying demonstrations in order to meet with those who might possibly be willing to buy our machine.

I negotiate for hours with La Compagnie Générale de Navigation Aérienne for the rights to build, sell or licence the use of the Wright flying machine in France. Last year, we came to Europe seeking a buyer, and did not find one. Now, the British say that they are interested, but would like to know more. Now the Germans say that they are interested, but would like to see the machine in operation.

It is like negotiating with pick-pockets; I will try to lose as little as I can.

Our agreement with the French is a bad bargain, but the only one that we felt that we could make. There has been no government which will agree to buy our machine. Without proof, they refuse to commit themselves; without a commitment, we have refused to fly.

Orville and I are very stubborn. We are the sons of Milton Wright. We will not give our secrets away without acknowledgement and reward. We will not be cheated of our due for what we have done.

"Is not your claim – that you have had very little practice time – your own fault, Monsieur Wright?"

"Should you not be flying, instead of tinkering with your machine?"

"If you had invented the machine that you claim to have invented, would you not be eager to demonstrate your claims?"

Picking through the broken bones of the Wright Flyer. Unpacking the cases in

Monsieur Bollée's shop. Prying the cases open with a crowbar. Shock at the bloody mess that the Flyer is in.

Lying on the cot in the shed which Monsieur Bollée has been kind enough to lend to me. Table, chair, wash basin, gas stove. The pieces of the Flyer at my elbow. I have refused to sleep in the nearby hotel.

Leafing through a stack of old newspapers in the evening. Coming across an interview with Octave Chanute.

"If the truth be known," the aging inventor proclaims, "it was myself who invented the term 'warping' for the method by which the Wright Brothers twist the wings of their machine in order to regain stability in the air."

The motor is revving up at optimum speed. The vibration is shaking the machine. Suddenly, I am being sprayed with boiling water. The rubber hose is slashing like a snake and spraying hot steam.

The broken ribs of the crated Flyer. Some of them splintered and needing replacement, not just repair. Everything in a shambles. Pieces scattered here and there among the broken bones of other things.

Sitting back on a stool in the shed and reading about the competition in the newspaper. A cup of coffee steaming on the bench.

"Leon Delagrange, in a machine of the Voisin Brothers' design, has flown for six minutes and thirty seconds, covering a distance of two and a half miles aloft in the air. Surely the age of flight is now at hand."

It has been five years since we flew at Kitty Hawk. Since that time, inventors have been working ceaselessly to duplicate the strides that we have made. The French have predicted that they would catch us, and surpass us, many times. But no one has flown with the kind of control that we have devised.

Our agreement with the French is not ideal.

We have agreed to demonstrate our flying machine in public. Two flights of thirty miles in an hour, with an ordinary wind. The second flight must be within two or three days of the first. We must carry a weight that corresponds to the weight of a passenger, with enough gasoline and water on board for a flight of at least 120 miles.

The Flyer is more than capable. It is not these details which are causing my sleepless nights.

"What is your answer, Monsieur Wright, to those who are calling you a coward?"

"Does it not worry you that other flyers – such as Farman, Delagrange and Blériot – are getting ahead of you?"

"Have you heard that Henri Farman is going to demonstrate his machine in New York?"

An angry letter to Orville.

"I opened the packing cases yesterday. I couldn't believe my eyes. The Flyer is smashed to smithereens. You must have used a scoop-shovel to throw everything into the boxes. Nothing was separated for safety. Did you ask Charlie to mix all of the part together so they wouldn't be lonesome?"

I wish that I was home.
At home, I would be helping father with his accounts. We would be searching for the elusive number – the red-handed digit – that would be trying to conceal a mountain of deceit. We would work all day at the figures, breaking off for lunch and supper, perhaps, but not letting those numbers have a rest 'til they have given up their yield.
In the evening though, the fireworks would draw us away.

I am burned across my bare arm. The water is pumping from the hose and slashing me across my bare arm at the elbow. It is blasting against my side. A stream of hot water is scalding me over my heart.

Icarus was stung. The branch swung back, as his father pushed it aside, and smacked him in the face.
Ouch, he thought, but didn't utter a sound. He didn't want his father to know that he had been following too closely again. My father is always right, he thought. He warned me not to follow so closely. No doubt, when I take my turn, and go first in the struggle, brushing aside the giant ferns that clog our path, my father will never walk so close that he will be slapped.

The Flyer has ten or eleven broken ribs. It's as if someone had taken a hammer to her. It is all the fault of Orville's packing. No care has been taken at all. There are no blocks to keep the parts from shifting around. It will be impossible to put back together quickly. The Flyer will take a very, very long time to re-create.

An angry letter to Orville.
"I can't believe you took two whole days to pack this machine! I could have done a better job in two or three minutes. How you could waste so much time just throwing things into the cases, I can't understand. You have failed miserably to do anything but cause a delay."

I raise my arm to protect my face. I stagger backwards and try to turn my face away. I feel the searing pain on the skin of my arm. Monsieur Bollée shouts for help and runs to my side.

Meetings, meetings, meetings.
For two and a half years, we did not test-fly our machine in order to protect our ideas from unscrupulous competitors. Now the British say that they will negotiate if we will demonstrate our ideas for all to see. Now the Germans promise a contract if we will fly our machine before the eyes of all the world.
I have given my word that the flying machine can do all that I say that it can do. Why will they not agree to a contract before I make a demonstration that will give our secrets away to all of our competitors?

Our agreement with the French is a terrible risk.
I have confidence in the Flyer, but there are many factors which could make her

fail the test. The weather, mechanical failure, a sudden gust of wind. The moment that I fly, we will be losing our secrets. In demonstrating our machine in France, I will be giving away our ideas to every unscrupulous pickpocket in the world.

"In what way, Monsieur Wright, have you modified the basic design of your illustrious mentor?"
"Why is Monsieur Chanute, himself, not here for the demonstration of his ideas?"
"Why did you not name the Wright Flyer the Flyer Chanute?"

There are darker days ahead.
For a number of years, Octave Chanute has been our ambassador to the French. By praising us, however, he has praised himself. By implying that we are his apprentices, he has taken much of the credit for our invention. Well, at least he used our name. At least the French are calling what has enabled them to fly "Le Système Wright" instead of "Le Système Octave Chanute".
All over France, inventors are flying with our ideas.

A tear formed in Icarus's eye. A thin sliver of the fern branch must have become lodged under his lid. He squinted and a tear ran down his cheek. He didn't stop to search for the sliver because he didn't want his father to know that he had been hurt.
He squinted, and faced the jungle with just one eye.
"Father," he called out. "You must be getting tired. I believe it must be my turn to take the lead."
He held his hand out in front of his closed eye. Another fern branch slapped against his arm.

The fabric is torn and hanging in a number of places. The aluminum paint has been scraped off the skids and has smeared on the cloth. Some of the ferrules will need to be re-soldered. Some of the uprights have no ferrules at all.

An angry letter to Orville.
"Where do you think that I am going to get replacement parts here in France? Do you realize that everything here has a different name than it has back home? Do you realize that everything here comes in different sizes? And many of the things are not available at all? Why couldn't you just pack the Flyer with a little more care?"

Sitting on the stool in the Flyer shed. Monsieur Bollée applying picric acid to my arm. A searing pain above my heart where I have been burned.

The radiator is punctured. The seat is all askew. The axle seems to be bent. The chain tubes are twisted. The propeller support is bent. There are no heavy wires bracing the ends of the heavy uprights.

"What proof do you offer, Monsieur Wright, for your claim to have flown successfully in 1903?"
"Why do you make these claims and offer no proof?"
"Is it perhaps because you have never flown at all?"

Sitting on the stool and sipping from a mug of coffee, with a folded piece of newspaper on my lap.

"Delagrange has remained airborne, here in Milan, for eighteen minutes and thirty seconds, covering a distance of nearly nine miles."

The competition flies and flops and flies again. They have no idea what they are inventing. They have no idea what works and what doesn't. Trial and error has no guarantees. What works in one lucky moment might be useless in the long run. Lucky moments are often un-recapturable. It is fine to guess at human flight, but we believe that it is far, far better to know.

An angry letter to Orville.

"And please tell me where are the missing bolts? Somewhere in the hold of the boat? Somewhere sitting on the dock? Maybe shipped back home to America? How did you think I was going to bolt the whole thing together?"

I wish I were at home.

At home, I would be helping Katharine and Orville and Lorin's children to decorate the house for the Fourth of July. On every post of the verandah we have a flag-holder which holds three little flags and Orville and I take turns lifting up the children and letting them put the little flags in the holders. When the whole house is decorated – when every flag is fluttering in the breeze – Katharine says it looks like a Mississippi river boat that is just about ready to up and sail away.

There is a blister on my arm. It is about a foot long and goes almost all the way around the arm. The burn on my side is about the size of my hand. The pain is very severe. Monsieur Bollée acted very quickly. The picric acid has certainly saved it from being worse.

The waves were tumbling on the shore. Icarus wiped the sleep that clogged his eyes. His father was sitting on the sand and watching the sea.
"What is it, father?"
"Just wait and you will see."
Just then, a white sail came around the edge of the cove.
"That sail is the latest patrol," Daedalus told him. "While you were asleep, I explored the cove. I also speared some fish. The King has the island surrounded with many sails."

Living alone, in a shed, in a country far from home; worrying about my brother being under attack from unfamiliar forces; pieces of our dream lying strewn around the floor; the broken and bent remains of a gleaming fact; straightening, fixing, repairing, while the competition seems to soar above my head; our mentor doling our life-blood out on every street-corner.

Blowing out the lantern and throwing myself, exhausted, onto the cot. There are times when I feel that everything is slowly and completely slipping away.

It is obvious what has happened. The vibration of the motor has caused the hose to work its way loose. More important than "what?" is "why?". This has never happened before. I grow careless when I work alone. When Orville and I are together, we are never complacent. Nothing is taken for granted. We always check and check, and then talk, and then check again.

The screws are the wrong size. The connecting-bolts are missing and so I cannot bolt the various sections together. I have no idea whether we can find anything to replace them. The fragments of the Wright Flyer are strewn all over the floor of Monsieur Bollée's shop. It will take a very long time to get everything back on track.

"Perhaps, Monsieur Wright, you can give me something to tell my editor, who is threatening, every day, to order me home?"
"Suppose you do fly, Monsieur Wright, what can you demonstrate that the others have not made familiar?"
"Claims of flight are not enough, Monsieur Wright; it seems that everyone can fly; can you show us anything that the others have not already done?"

There are darker days ahead.
Since 1906, when we secured the patents, we have been unable to protect our ideas. Orville and I were twenty years ahead of all of the other inventors in 1903. But now, thanks to Octave Chanute, we are only five. Now, we have no patent protection in France. Anyone if France can build a Wright-style flying machine simply by looking at the American patent that we have secured.

An angry letter to Orville.
"You cannot just leave things loose inside the packing crates and hope for the best. You must realize that breakable items must be packed inside smaller boxes and then these boxes must be placed inside larger boxes. Things must be done ten times better next time than they were this time. The time you spent packing was entirely wasted. I could have smashed the Flyer with a hammer myself and saved you the time."

Sitting on my cot in the shed of Monsieur Bollée. A break in a grinding day. The coffee is hot, but bitter. Opening a letter from Octave Chanute.
"I cannot urge you strongly enough that I think that you are making a mistake. I insist that you not offer your machine abroad until you are sure that every avenue of opportunity has been exhausted for the sale of this invention to our own government. Your invention is too important to allow it to get away. Would you want it on your conscience if the value of this machine should be in the control of hostile hands?"

I am afraid that Orville will be distracted by the crowds, the military observers, and the demands of the newspapermen, who want more than they are entitled to ask anyone to give. I wish that I had never left him to face these hostile forces by himself.
Neither Orville nor I should ever work alone. We never should have agreed to separate.

I wish I were at home.
There would be no nicer way to spend the day than for Orv and I to get our bicycles out and to pack a picnic lunch and to ride way out to the Pinnacles, where it all started. We could just lie back in the long grass and watch the hawks circle lazily in the

up-draughts. That was where the whole idea of human flight began.

For just five minutes of being at home, I would trade the whole two months I've been in France.

I wake up in a sweat. It is the middle of the night. The workers of Monsieur Bollée will not arrive until an hour after dawn. I turn the lantern on. I turn on the gas and light the stove. I put the coffee on to boil. I turn and face the parts of the Flyer that are laid out on the floor.

Daedalus picked up a stick that was lying on the beach.

"We must abandon the idea of a raft," he said. "The king controls the land and patrols the sea. There is only one element over which he has set no guards."

He took the stick and began to draw a diagram in the sand.

"I have been thinking all my life of the flight of man," Daedalus said, as he added a curve that connected two other lines. "I told King Minos when I built the labyrinth: 'the greatest prisons are the cradles for the greatest thoughts'." He scuffed a line out with his foot and took the stick and scratched a replacement line. "The king ignored my comment, but I will prove him wrong to have done so. I know, now, what we will do. We will make wings and fly far over the walls of our jail."

"Do you think, Monsieur Wright, that you will ever be ready to fly?"

I must warn Orville to be sure to check the hose. If it is unnoticed, it will work its way loose. The blistering is very severe. With this pain, I can hardly move. The newspapers will have a field-day. They will say that I am stalling for time. With these burns, there will be no flying for quite a while.

Chapter 6
Orville Wright 2

Fort Myer, Virginia
September 2, 1908

A dull day at Fort Myer.
The flying machine is in the balloon house. The frame is assembled and the wings are being sown. Then I will be able to string the wires. The gasoline tank holds about twelve or thirteen gallons. That's seventy pounds of gasoline.

Apollo sat on his throne. His robe was purple and his crown was gold, and the throne was glittering with a thousand points of light. Around Apollo lounged a dazzling array of persons. Perhaps, Phaeton thought, they might be gods.
"The Day, The Month, The Year", Apollo boomed, and each time he spoke, a figure bowed. Each one had a wrinkled face and was very old. "The Hours", Apollo said, and waved at a group of figures with pointed hats. Many, but not all of them, gestured back. "Spring, Summer, Autumn, Winter," the voice boomed out. "I'm sure you have met them all before. It is these who are my assistants in providing time."

The nightmares never cease.
It is five long years since the first flight at Kitty Hawk, and we are not yet out of the woods.
The fear of making a mistake. No one can realize how many factors there are in the act of lifting the flying machine off the ground. There are so many things that can go wrong.
It is agony trying to think of everything when I am alone.

"Why is your brother not taking part in your demonstrations for the Army, Mr. Wright?"
"Why has your mentor, Octave Chanute, stayed away?"
"How can one man, alone, do what the most eminent engineers and scientists of our society – with all of their financial resources and expertise – could not accomplish?"

I worry about Wilbur being alone.

He has scalded himself with hot water from a hose. He forgot to tighten the hose and the pressure built up and the hot steam exploded and he scalded his arm.

Wilbur tells me very little, but the newspapers tell me that he is badly burned.

I will have to ask Katharine if she has more details. Perhaps he has been candid with her. Wilbur says that I shouldn't mention it when I write.

I miss the family back at home.

At home, it would be Father on his rocker on the porch, Katharine in her wicker chair, and Wilbur and I lolling on the swing, dreaming up the most fantastic plans for something that has only been dreamed about for thousands of years.

Practical plans for the nuts and bolts of a thousand-year-old dream.

It is hard to work with people always watching you. The Army has people constantly watching. They feel it is their right to view the machine. It is hard when you feel the need to scratch your head and wonder what to do. It is important to always look positive. They would be surprised if they knew how often Wilbur and I have to stop for a while and talk things over before we figure out what we are going to do next. I have two mechanics here, Charlie Furnas and Charlie Taylor, but it isn't the same as having Wilbur to complete my thought each time I stop and scratch my head.

Settling into the Cosmo Club in Washington. The reading room, after dinner, is a restful place.

The newspapers on the table catch my eye.

"The Red Wing, the flying machine which has been designed by Glenn Curtiss, has managed to fly. It flew for nineteen seconds and stayed in the air for three hundred and nineteen feet. Surely the age of human flight has finally arrived."

Phaeton glanced at the flowers, the grain, the grape-juice and the hoar frost, and moved a little farther away from Winter.

Apollo leaned down from his throne and cupped his ear. "And now, young fellow, please tell me how I can help you. What is it that you have come here to request?"

The Fort Myer parade ground is very small. Only seven hundred by a thousand feet. That doesn't give me much time to get air-borne. Not much room to recover from a mistake. Much smaller than the field where we usually fly, but it will have to do. The Army doesn't consider that these are the conditions for a miracle. They have contracted for a practical flying machine.

"But a bicycle shop, Mr. Wright?"

"And in rural Dayton, Ohio, and remoter Kitty Hawk?"

"Is all of this not a stunt just to sell your bicycles?"

A conciliatory letter to Wilbur.

"I can imagine your shock as you opened the packing crates. I am sorry for what happened to the Flyer, but you don't seem to understand. The packing crates were packed as carefully as you would have done them yourself. Every item was treated as if it was made of glass."

I have gone over the grounds for five miles in several directions from the Fort. That gives me a chance to map the most advantageous flying plan. Perhaps the best route will be to fly directly towards Alexandria. Five miles out and five miles back. It is over a large woods, a mile in width, to be sure, with no breaks from start to finish. But there are some landing places on either side. Fort Myer is 240 feet above sea level. The turning point is 160 feet. Three deep ravines will have to be crossed. The lowlands are ploughed and would make the best place for an emergency landing.

Sitting in my room at the Cosmo Club in Washington. The view from my window is all that I could ask.

Sitting at the desk and catching up on my mail. Opening a letter from Octave Chanute.

"I must warn you as a friend. Do you not realize that while you are perfecting your invention under wraps, the rest of the world is catching up to you? Others are making flying machines. Others are learning to fly. I urge you to lower your price and sign a contract for your machine. I realize that secrecy is important, but the lengths to which you are going are absurd. Your secrets will be worth nothing if others succeed."

Our competitors are ignoring the legality of the patents that we have obtained. Their strategy is to make money from our invention while we are fighting in the courts. Each time we win a decision, they will alter their machines and go on selling them. Then we are forced to start the legalities over again. There is nothing they can devise that is not covered in the patent for our machine.

The difficult thing will be in the testing of the machine. I want to get in a lot of practice, if I can. I need to get used to the machine while being watched by my observers. Any mishaps in practice will convince them that the Flyer won't fly. The parade ground is very small for flying a machine. The five-man jury is very irritating to me. They watch the preparations, but they don't let on what they are thinking. The newspaper men are friendly, but Professor Langley's failures have prepared them for disappointment. I can tell that none of them expects the Flyer to be able to fly.

Phaeton cleared his throat. He was very, very dry. It had been a long walk up the mountain and he had waited a very long time for the gate-keeper to appear.

Then he had climbed the palace steps. There were many guards on the steps, and many more on the landings. It was hot and it was dry, but none of them had offered him a drink.

"O great god, Apollo," Phaeton said, as his mother had taught him patiently to do. She had made up a little speech and had him say it over and over until she felt that he had it memorized just right. "My name is Phaeton. I have permission to be absent from school. I have come here to ask you to confirm that you are my father. My mother, Clymene, has told me of three great things: that you are my father, that you never tell a lie, and that you are bound to grant your son whatever he should wish."

"Is this not an age-old illusion, Mr. Wright?"
"Has man not dreamed, in futility, for a thousand years?"
"Surely, Mr. Wright, you can be candid and agree that what you propose is not

within the realm of human possibility?"

A conciliatory letter to Wilbur.
"All of the lids on the packing crates were secured with screws. This was to allow the French Customs Officers access so they could restore the lids when they were finished with their inspection. All of the parts were fastened securely so they wouldn't bounce around. Every item was packed separately to ensure that it would remain safe."

I miss the family back at home.
At home, it would be tea-time on the porch. The family rule of no reading while the tea and cake are being served. The agony of trying to break away from the friendly argument between Wilbur and I – about the curvature of the wing, say, or about an equation for the amount of lift in our new design – to simply be civilized enough to say hello to a visiting neighbour.

Running the engine on the track out on the parade ground. Tuning it up to the smoothness that I know I will need to fly. My group of observers is convinced that I am wasting their valuable time. Everyone has become an expert on the flying machine. A few years ago, when Professor Langley was so confident, and the Army gladly gave him money to pursue his dreams, no one knew anything about the possibility of human flight. They looked to the professor for expertise in an unknown field. Now, five years after the Professor tried and failed, everyone has become an expert on the topic of aviation. They are all quite versed in failure. They have all lined the Potomac, with the flags flying and the band playing, expecting flight and finding failure, and it has made them feel that they know the subject well.

A long, cold, bitter day. Exhausted at the Cosmo Club in Washington. Barely energy enough to read the article that is pointed out to me.
An article in the Scientific American.
"Glenn Curtiss is offering flying machines for sale, for a price of five thousand dollars each."

The gods all looked at Apollo. Apollo looked amused. Then his face broke into a grin. Then the other gods all grinned. Then Apollo looked very smug and then he spoke: "I am the god Apollo. Your mother has taught you well. She spoke wisely when she told you of the three great truths. I am your father, my son. And no, I never tell a lie. And I am prepared to grant you anything under the sun."
Then Apollo grinned and everybody laughed.

It is 1908. Five years after the Langley fiasco. Now, the experts gather in small groups and ignore me as I work. Now, they reluctantly leave their tasks and report to the parade ground to take the mandatory glance at the latest attempt to bamboozle the government. At the carnival salesman with the contraption that will raise lead into the air and make it fly, defying all of the proven properties of matter and gravity. Now, they huddle in small groups and glance at me and talk of anything but the matter at hand. They are all experts in the impossibility of human flight.

"Have you incorporated aspects of the Langley Aerodrome, Mr. Wright?"

"Do you believe Professor Langley's claim that he was only inches away from taking flight?"

"What parts of your machine would you attribute to the contribution of Mr. Chanute?"

A conciliatory letter to Wilbur.

"All of the goods came here, to Washington, in perfect shape. They were packed in exactly the same way as the goods that were shipped to France. It was not the fault of the packing that the Flyer suffered injury. It was the simple fact that the French Customs Officers did not know, or did not care, that the contents in the packing crates were so very fragile. It was they who put the parts in the boxes with a scoop-shovel."

Running the engine sure turns up some interesting things. Chains, cases and thrust rods will have to be loosened and re-aligned. The bronze bearings for the thrust rods seem to be bent. The engine keeps stopping. This has happened twice. The bearings are running too hot for me to fly. Maybe it's the gasoline that is causing the engine to skip. I'll have to try a higher octane and see how she runs.

A conciliatory letter to Wilbur.

"Naturally, I regret the time-delay. It is unfortunate that the language is a barrier. It is unfortunate that some parts are not available over there. Nevertheless, I am amazed at your resilience. You are coping amazingly well. You will forget these setbacks the moment you are in the air."

I miss the family back at home.

At home, it would be our brother-Lorin's children, dropping into the bicycle shop and admiring the new bicycles that have just arrived from the manufacturer. Maybe Wilbur and I taking them out for a quick spin, balancing them one-at-a-time on the crossbar, cradled in our arms, as we tour a few blocks of West Third Street.

Sitting at a desk in the Cosmo Club in Washington, after a long day of preparation of our machine. Almost too tired to dip the pen in the ink and write.

I am sending a letter to L'Aérophile, the aeronautical magazine. It is important to make the legalities of our patents well-known, to link them to our name, so that everyone will be aware that our competitors are stealing. It is important to point out that our methods are not those of Octave Chanute, and that our patent is very specific as to what we have done. It is important that we be given credit for what we have achieved.

Bad luck. The Flyer has jumped herself right off the track. Just a practice run, but, still, a bad moment. The soldiers were turning the Flyer around when the truck slid off the track and the wing hit the ground. No damage that I can see, but not a good sign. I cannot see any damage, but I will be cautious. I will go over every part of the machine before I bring her out again. I am sure that this wouldn't have happened if the two of us had both been here. The others are very helpful, but I am sorry that I need their help. Wilbur and I never let anyone but ourselves touch the machine.

Phaeton looked up at his new-found father. Apollo leaned down from his throne and smiled at his son.

"And now, what is it you request, young man? I assure you that I remember your mother well. I used to meet her in the garden. We had many fine conversations in our time." Apollo grinned and the other gods all smiled. "There is nothing that I would refuse a son of mine."

"Well, Father," Phaeton said. "Since you will deny me no request, I would like to drive the Chariot of the Sun."

"Will you defy the laws of gravity, Mr. Wright?"

"Will you overcome the properties of matter with your machine?"

"Do you mean to tell us, Mr. Wright, that you are about to inaugurate a whole new era for all of mankind?"

A conciliatory letter to Wilbur.

"Charlie and I are packing as carefully as we have ever done before. We are also including a sign, in both English and French this time, asking please – s'il vous plaît – return the contents to their original situations of security. We can only hope that the French Customs Officers will be willing to comply."

Testing the machine. Another piece of bad luck. A rope has broken, dropping four hundred pounds of iron down from the derrick, skinning the chin of First Lieutenant Creecy, USMC. I feel for the lieutenant. I have been where he has been. Bruises and scrapes on the chin are a necessary part of the trade.

Riding back to the Cosmo Club in Washington. Wondering what is in my pocket that I had forgotten about.

I had forgotten another letter from Octave Chanute.

"I must warn you of approaching doom. Farman, in France, has turned a circle. No matter that it is clumsy. It is a circle, nevertheless. You are relying too much on your assumption of your own superiority. For now, you have the lead, but there are no secrets in the sky that are reserved for only you. You are smug if you think that you can take your time and perfect your machine while expecting others to take no advantage of your delay. You are in danger of losing everything that you have worked for."

Every god looked at Apollo. Apollo looked at his son. Apollo's face fell and his eyes went blank and then a small smile creased the corner of his mouth.

"My son jests," he said, and a few gods smiled. "Or perhaps I have heard him wrong." Apollo cupped his ear and leaned down from his throne. "Phaeton," he said, "I am sure I have misunderstood. Would you be so kind as to clarify your request?"

Wilbur has burned himself, quite severely, with scalding water from a hose. He tells me very little, but the newspapers tell me that Wilbur is badly burned. This would never have happened, I am sure, if I had been there. We always check each other's work and then check again.

Neither Wilbur nor I should ever work alone. We never should have agreed to separate.

"Would you agree that your machine looks as ready as it will ever be, Mr. Wright?"

Making adjustments as I go. I have better friction on the levers for the wing-tips and the rudder. That should give me the tension that I desire. But now the engine is missing explosions. It shows up in the smell of gasoline and a change in the exhaust. The engine refuses to deliver speed. The contract with the Army specifies an average speed of forty miles per hour. Perhaps I can make a change. I will concentrate on the octane, the oil cups and the magneto and hope for enough improvement to meet the requirement. The observers turn away and test the air for the coming rain. They have mentally filed their reports of the latest fiasco. The soldiers too are bored, but I must ask them to move the machine back into the balloon shed. I must get all of these problems solved before I can fly.

Chapter 7
The Wright Brothers 3

Kitty Hawk, North Carolina
December 17, 1903

A busy day at Kitty Hawk.
Ten thirty. Not too bad. Thirty minutes of fitting together and we have ourselves a flying machine. Main frame, tail frame, front rudder frame and surfaces. Fitting together just as smoothly as we could wish. She looks good sitting there on the launch-rail. A few drops of gasoline pumped into each cylinder. Hoist the battery box onto the wing and hook her up to the engine. Hope there's nothing we didn't notice. You can look her over a thousand times and still not be sure. One of us at each propeller. "Ready! Set! Go!" Double-spin and the engine coughs and jumps to life.

Prometheus thrashed his way through the underbrush. Thorns and nettles scratched at his thighs. Branches slashed him in the face. He held his hands out in front to protect his eyes. The ground was sloping and uncertain but he couldn't see past his waist. The branches closed in as soon as he brushed them aside.
Olympus was always busy. There would probably be many gods. It was mid-way through the morning. If he kept a steady pace, he would be able to arrive sometime near noon. He was counting on the rumours that the gods didn't work all day. He had heard that they often had an afternoon sleep.

There is always something more. Another problem, another need, among a flurry of problems that the others still haven't encountered. Success has put us in a place that is new and strange. When we glide longer and farther than the others have managed to do, we end up in a place where the problems of human flight seem to multiply. For every solution that we come up with, there is another dilemma just waiting to spring out of the air and challenge us.

Forces, pressures, natural phenomena, human response. A cloud of numbers, concepts, equations. The water that we swim in; the air we breathe. Why have these secrets been waiting for so long? Waiting for us to reach up and pluck them out of the sky?

Vertical rudder - twelve square feet - six feet height - double-fin arrangement - constant control - pin-wheeling motion - thirty two feet by five feet - three hundred and five square feet - seven degrees - one eighth of the weight.

Kitty Hawk is cold in mid-December, all right, but is the finest place in the world to visit in autumn. Kitty Hawk has been home for us for four years during the gliding season.

Every year since 1900, in September, when the bicycle season is over, we say goodbye to Father and Katharine and Lorin and the children and set off on the train from Dayton to Elizabeth City, North Carolina, then by boat across Albemarle Sound to Kitty Hawk. We have learned to bring everything we need. Kitty Hawk is a sandbar and it is difficult to obtain here what is readily available in Dayton, Ohio. If we need parts for our gliders, we are forced to obtain them from home.

Kitty Hawk is the best place we could find to practice our gliding. Kitty Hawk is the beach and the tumbling waves. Kitty Hawk is sand and wind and sun. Kitty Hawk is standing on Big Kill Devil Hill at sunrise and watching the sun lighting up the entire Atlantic Ocean.

Warm-up. Shuddering on the rail. Clamped to the bench with a c-clamp. Threatening to shake herself loose from the bench where the wing is leaning. "Keep an eye on her." "Don't let the wing shake herself loose from the bench and drop down into the sand." Running her a couple of minutes. Watching the engine and propellers. Letting them work out the kinks. Just a little exercise to get them in working order. It was the misfiring of the engine that caused the vibrations that did us in before. Running smoothly now. Hope she holds.

Why would this be happening? The wing warping has been working so well. When we lose equilibrium, we warp the wing-tips – one wing-tip up and one wing-tip down – so the machine regains its equilibrium again. This has been working very well. So why would something new be happening to us now?

Fore and aft control - end controls - excessive twist - side sway - sticks in a heap - wind velocity - wing-twisting - amount of practice - boisterous winds - broken spars and ribs.

Kitty Hawk is the people.

The fellows of the Life Saving Station at Kill Devil Hills, who plunge into the Atlantic in all seasons and all weathers, whenever a shipwreck occurs. They have been good enough to come up here to the camp whenever we tack the red flag on the side of the shed to help us do our gliding.

And Bill Tate, who took us into his house when we first came here, and has been very helpful showing us the ropes around here ever since. Who is post-master, farmer, fisherman and politician of Kitty Hawk and who tries to do his day's work in two or three hours so he can spare the time to come over and help us fly our machines.

It was noon. The sun was overhead and Leonardo was at the highest possible spot that his climbing of the morning would allow. All Florence was below him; above him, a golden eagle soared on the currents of the air.

He stopped climbing and sat down on a piece of rock.

A bird is no more, or less, magnificent than my hand, he thought. He put his hand down on the rock and looked at it for a while. Light and shadow on the surface of a fine machine. Then he held the hand up, about a foot in front of his eyes and flexed it and relaxed it – back and forth. He tried to look right through the flesh at what he had seen during dissections many times. Then he let the sinews and the veins and the skin come back into his field of vision.

He eased the bag, with the notebook and the loaf of bread, down beside the rock on which he was sitting.

With such a machine as this hand – the practical functioning of a miracle of complexity – we will someday hover in the air.

Numbers, numbers, numbers. 351 revolutions per minute. About five revolutions per second. 132 pounds of thrust. The machine is shuddering on the rails. Octave Chanute said we'd lose from twenty-five to thirty percent of our power from the motor to the air. Our calculations show we only lose about fifteen percent. The machine is eager to take to the air. Very soon we will know which set of numbers is correct.

When we attempt to make a turn to the left, the turn will start just fine – a gentle curving motion to the left – but then there comes a point where the machine will stop and completely reverse direction. The machine will turn back to the right instead of the left. A complete loss of control. Now what on earth would be the cause of that?

We are ahead of all of the others. None of them has ever turned a flying machine in the air. None of them has even been forced to figure out the science of turning a flying machine while in flight. We are encountering phenomena that the others have not even wondered at. Things are happening in the air that couldn't be guessed.

Vertical axis - positive warp - drag - side motion - pivoting motion - vertical fins - rotation about the axis - movable fins - vertical rudders - five feet height.

Kitty Hawk is sand. Acres and acres and acres of wind-blown sand. The sea and the wind conspire to wash hundreds and hundreds of loads of sand ashore in heaps along the coast. There are four hills of sand near our camp and they are perfect to launch our gliders from. The sand is a soft cushion for bumpy landings.

The sand is quite ubiquitous. It rattles on the windows and makes little piles as it seeps in through the cracks in the door.

Shaking the sand out of the pages of the newspaper and smoothing them out on the table. Then sitting down to read with a cup of coffee.

The newspaper reporters seem to love Professor Langley. They follow the learned Professor in eager swarms.

"I have every confidence," says Professor Langley," that today will be a very special day. We have set our houseboat here, in the Potomac River, as a means of demonstrating publicly that human flight is well within our grasp. The study of aeronautics is the most rewarding field of scientific investigation which remains to us, and holds the promise of future military and commercial benefits for mankind. No, sir, I'm not worried about what today will bring at all. I have every confidence that the Langley

Aerodrome will fly."

Better, of course, to have tested the Flyer as a glider. Better, we still believe, to have tested the size, weight and shape of the new machine in flight conditions without the motor. Better to learn to use the new controls when only powered by the wind. But the confidence of Professor Langley has stampeded us. Has made us move our plans ahead. He has made us leap-frog over the days that we would have spent testing and improving our machine. He has made us pole-vault over the methods by which we have done our work so far.

Prometheus danced his way upward on the shale. At times, he fell down and slid back down the slope. His elbows were cut and bleeding and his knees were slashed and bruised. It was blazing hot in the full sun of the summer.
He had been to Mount Olympus before, but he was still unsure of the way. In his anger, the other time, he had brutalized his way past every obstacle. Now, he felt cold inside. He knew what he wanted to do and he had decided to do it. It would be the last day of the old era for both man and the gods.

There is a need to understand why the turns reverse. When turning the machine, we warp the wings. We raise the tip of one wing, and lower the tip of the other wing, creating a lift that raises one side of the machine. So far, this is logical and fine. The machine starts the turn, and goes smoothly for a while, but why does it so suddenly turn against us?

Vertical fins - slippage - vertical surfaces - turning sideways - yawing from side to side - crosswinds - stability of the machine - an unseen force - pitch control - well-digging.

Kitty Hawk is the sunsets.
Deep blue clouds all fringed with gold. And the clouds light up with all colours in the background. All night the moon lights up the sand as if it was day. You can read your watch by the starlight shining on the canvas of the tent.
God's world is basic here. Out here there is just the sand and the sky and the ocean.

The vibration of the propellers has settled down. Vibration is very strong at lower speeds. Chilly in the mornings. Ponds of ice all around our camp. Every puddle is a slippery sheet. Hope there are no slips while we are running beside the machine. The northern wind is very cold. The sprockets are holding very well. The Arnstein's hard cement has taken care of the loosening problem. Doubt if those sprockets will ever shake themselves loose again.

Leonardo sat on the rock and watched the birds.
A golden eagle searched around for wind currents. When it found one, it soared for many miles.
A bird is an instrument working according to mathematical law, which instrument it is within the capacity of man to reproduce with all its movements, though not with its strength. The great mystery is in how the bird maintains equilibrium. That is what

I am concerned to discover today. Close and constant observation is the key to all significant understanding.

It is inconceivable that man cannot do everything that a bird can do. We must study birds in order to study man. If every problem raises the question of the definition of the essence of man, then every solution must expand that definition.

The problem then, is this: while the rising wing creates a lift, it also creates a drag. The drag slows the wing speed of the higher wing in the air. Then the lower wing goes faster than the higher wing, causing the lower wing to suddenly move ahead and turn the flying machine away from the turn, back in the direction that it has come from. All of this is clear enough, but what to do about it is now the perplexing question. Our experience in the air is now outdistancing our theory. What is needed to stop this uncontrolled reversal?

Weight of standard air - net speed - volume of air - gross speed - 20 gauge steel - thickened front edges - fore and aft dimension - upper surface - angle of advance - slope of six degrees.

Kitty Hawk is birds.

Buzzards, eagles, ospreys. Hen hawks and pigeons. Mockingbirds and red-birds and brown thrashers and sparrows and wrens. Watching them and wondering. Noting their strengths and their weaknesses. Noting which of them fares best in the buffeting winds.

Eagles and hawks fare better in stronger winds than buzzards do. It has to do with the shape of the wings. Dihedral for the buzzards; anhedral for the eagles and the hawks.

Seagulls skimming the waves. Sea chickens hoping about on one foot as they hunt on the beach. Standing outside the shed and watching an eagle flapping its wings far up in the distance.

The world that they live in will soon be shared by man.

We have solved the problem of lateral motion, with our wing warping. We have solved the problem of lift with the curve of our wings.

Now, how to solve the problem of the reverse slide? How to overcome the loss of control when in the middle of a turn? How to stop the machine from resisting the operator and refusing control?

Unexpected winds - depth perception - 160 feet - 200 feet - sidling effect - sliding backwards - tailspin - fixed vertical fins - banking the wings - sideslip.

Octave Chanute was very cold. He warmed his hands at the fire. We had told him that we were within days of being ready to attempt the first powered human flight.

"I have always encouraged you," he said. "I have promoted your work throughout the scientific community. When I saw that you were having such success with your gliders, I encouraged you to come and speak to the Western Society of Civil Engineers, in Chicago. I introduced you as having made a significant contribution to the knowledge of human flight. It was in this way that I have encouraged appreciation of all that you have done."

Shaking the sand out of the newspaper in the warmth of the shed.

Forty miles south of Washington, on a houseboat on the Potomac River. The newspapers report the launch of Professor Langley's air machine.

"Easily and rapidly the mechanical bird moved along the seventy foot track. The speed was not great, apparently not more than forty or fifty feet a second. It took the air fairly well. For a fraction of a second, the Aerodrome stood up in the face of the five-mile wind then blowing. But when that brief period had passed, there had passed also the time when the airship had a chance for successful flight. The next instant the big and curious thing turned gradually downward."

Foolish to worry about Professor Langley. We shouldn't have changed our schedule because of him. The professor has not studied the birds. His wings are shaped like those of a buzzard. Ours are shaped like those of a gull. He has not noticed that a gull can fly in the strongest winds while a buzzard cannot. Still, trial and error can sometimes lead to surprising success.

Leonardo leaned back on the rock and studied the birds.

The sun was bright, and he squinted, but his sight was as clear as it had been when he was eighteen. With age, the mind grows better at understanding what younger eyes can only wonder at.

A golden eagle was soaring in the wind.

I will reduce the number of lines in which I capture what I see. From outside to essence with each successive sketch. I will capture what I see when I seize the bird in the air, and freeze him in my gaze, and let the sunlight penetrate his feathers and his skin. This requires the rendering of less and less of the detail that I have observed. I must reduce my drawings to the most basic lines of all – the shape of the body and the configuration of the wings.

In this way, I will learn the lessons that are hidden in the air.

Talk and thought and talk. Even arguing, as we have always done. What if this? What if that? What to try? What to discard? What to add to the machine or what to take away?

But change is never simple. Change is never single. When one thing changes, everything else will change. To make one change is to make a whole new flying machine.

Excessive cups of coffee. Late nights spent sleepless in pursuit of the unperceived glint of breakthrough logic. Like looking under the sofa for the missing puzzle-piece.

Fourteen inches front to back - control and balance - deadly spin - course of flight - maximum crosswind - controlled descent - front rudder - pressure from below - relative wind - nine to eleven metre winds.

For us, Kitty Hawk has been gliding.

Four years of theories and building and practice. Four years of stretching seconds in the air into minutes. Four years of scraped chins and black eyes and broken piles of wood and wire. Four years of landing in a heap and picking ourselves out of the wreckage. Four years of carrying the pieces back to the camp and starting again.

But four years, too, of planning and building a succession of kites and gliders that have brought us closer and closer to the attainment of our dream. Four years of soaring from the sides of the sand hills and catching the winds that blow in from the Atlantic and lift our wings.

Every year at Kitty Hawk we have moved closer to the achievement of human flight.

Setting up the camera on the tripod. "Sorry John. No exercise for you." "You'll have to stand here shivering in the cold." "She should lift off the ground about forty feet along the track." "That's about two-thirds of the way along." "Any wind above twenty miles an hour will make her lift just about there." "Just want to catch her as she lifts herself up and into the air."

Prometheus paused and leaned on a crag. The sweat was pouring off him and his cuts and scrapes were sore. A trickle of blood was streaked across his arm. He hadn't thought to bring any water. It had been awhile since he'd encountered a mountain stream.

Above him, catching an up-draught, a golden eagle soared lazily around and around. It was interesting to think about. The eagle was a bird. The birds were subject to the gods. How was it then that the eagle, any time he wanted to, could flap his wings and soar higher than Mount Olympus?

The sun broke through the clouds and the ice was glinting on the puddles. It was a warm spell, and Octave Chanute came out of the tent and watched us work.

"I offered to put you in touch with Andrew Carnegie," he said. "I offered to give you a personal recommendation. I said that there are a number of wealthy men who would like to connect their names with something as forward-looking as the possibility of flight. I offered to secure a stipend for you of ten thousand dollars per year, so you could continue to do exactly as you do. I felt it would help to put you on a more sound financial basis. It would free you from the burden of the bicycle shop. There would be no obligation except to continue the precious work that you are doing. I was surprised when you turned my offer down. I have often wondered at your penchant for working alone."

Finally, an answer seems to take shape: if the problem is that the low wing moves ahead of the high wing during a turn, why not slow the movement of the low wing as it moves forward?

We have had a fixed vertical tail and we have had problems. Why not have a movable rudder that slows down the low-wing speed, and prevents the machine from sliding ahead on the lower side? We will try it in the morning: perhaps a movable vertical rudder will help us to regain what has slipped away from us. Tomorrow we will try to regain our control of the air.

Kitty Hawk is hot biscuits and eggs and tomatoes. Coffee and butter and bacon and corn bread. Kitty Hawk is good eating in season when the winds permit the boats to come over from the mainland, and near-starvation when the supplies run low and we are forced to live without hot drink or bread or crackers.

Kitty Hawk is buying supplies at Mr. Calhoun's store and a chat with an old fellow, at the counter, face worn with the years of wresting fish from Atlantic storms.

Fingernails blackened and knuckles knurled as they cradle a can of beans.

"God give man legs. God give man arms. And he give him ears a nose and teeth" – a closer lean and an almost imperceptible wink – "and a lot of other things which I ain't going to mention" – the fingers curling tightly around the can of beans – "but I never seen a man yet who was born with wings."

"There was a roaring, grinding noise and the Langley airship tumbled over the edge of the houseboat and disappeared into the river, sixteen feet below," the newspapers reported – objectively of course, but with a just a tiny hint of reporterly glee. "It simply slid into the water like a handful of mortar."

"A boy is given a golden bridle," Katharine says. "A gift, without a warning, from the gods." She is taking a break from her lesson plans. The four of us on a winter evening. The fireplace in the parlour is as warm as toast. "The boy approaches the magnificent horse as it is drinking at a well, and holds the bridle out in front of him, and Pegasus whinnies softly and approaches the boy and allows himself to be tamed. The boy then mounts the prancing steed, and Pegasus opens out the span of his magnificent wings and gallops along the ridge and leaps into the air."

"John, all you have to do is to squeeze this bulb." "That's all you have to do." "That'll snap the shutter open and closed and we'll have ourselves a picture." Inserting the glass-plate negative. "But you'll have to snap it fast." Adjusting the lens. We want the probable lift-off point to be about the centre of the photograph. "In practice, the machine covered the last fifteen feet in one and a half seconds, so there's not going to be much time." Something seems to be wrong. "John, what's the matter?" Knit brow and worried eyes. "John, what's the matter? Have you never taken a photograph before?

Chapter 8
Wilbur Wright 3

Le Mans, France
August 8, 1908

Another long day in France.
Ready to fly at last. Everything appears to be in order, though, without Orville, I cannot be sure. A small crowd has gathered. A few hundred of the curious. There have been so many delays and so many charges of fraud that there are very few here who believe that a Wright can fly.

"Why did the gods not make us capable of flying, Father?" asked Icarus, as his father ground up the ingredients that would make the wax. He ground them in the hollow of a stone.
"On the contrary, my son, I believe that they have done so."
"Done so, father? But we have no wings."
"No, but we have been given the capacity to fly, nevertheless. I have come to believe, throughout the years, that the gods do not come with their gifts and place them on our laps, like surprises. On the contrary, if we are to enjoy the benefits of life on the earth we must take them for our use from the laps of the gods."

There is no difference between the night and the day. What pokes and prods me during the night, and what disturbs me during the day, is the nightmare nature of what my life has now become.
I am sure that for Orville it has become the same.

"May we see the wound, Monsieur Wright?"
"If your claims of a need for a delay are to be believed, Monsieur Wright, you must show us the wound."
"Was there actually an accident, Monsieur Wright, or is it a convenient fabrication to justify your delay?"

Orville and I have become part of a great whirlpool of speculation, rumour, commentary, editorial opinion, hope and cynicism. There are those who believe in us, and those who disbelieve in us; those who promote us and those who compete with us; those who wish us well and those who dismiss us.

There is a significant group who are watching and noting today who would gladly steal from us.

Orville and I are prisoners of the hopes and fears of the public mind. Our every move is on display at the public zoo. I lie awake and think of the danger of my pockets being picked; I fall asleep and dream about the same.

The machine seems to be humming. A number of last-minute preparations. There is never enough time to get things right. I put on the 1904 propellers with the appropriate sprockets. They seem to be running well without too much advance of the spark.

"But is flight not stealing from the gods, Father?" asked Icarus, as his father stirred the wax.

"Only time itself can reveal the consequences, of course," replied Daedalus, "but I suspect that the gods place gifts in their laps to test us. I am inclined to believe that the gods have smiled in the past when they have been witness to the audacity of Man."

Icarus felt the warmth of the sand on his soles. As the sun rose higher, he would have to walk carefully, as he gathered the necessary materials for his father. Without sandals, perhaps the sun would burn his feet.

"Why has the arm taken so long to heal, Monsieur Wright?"
"Surely your arm has healed enough for you to fly?"
"Is this not just one more excuse for your delay?"

I worry about Orville being alone.

The pressure is intense. There is a barrage of questions every time I appear in public. I wonder how he is handling the relentless attention.

I wish that I were at home.

At home, I would be helping Father in the endless adventure of tracking the missing numbers across the sand-hills of his copy of the account books. Engaged in the adventure of cornering the moustache-twirling varmint who has had his way with the numbers of the Church of the United Brethren. Proving that the innocent-seeming column of numbers is the false prop of a corrupt financial scheme.

An evening of adventure – with my blood-hound of a pen – searching for villains in the sand-hills of father's accounts.

The men run outward to prime the catapult. A signal from me and they let the weight go and I spring forward and into the air. I cannot hear a gasp from the crowd, but I can feel it. No lumbering down the field and bumping over cow-patties. The French are amazed that the Flyer can jump so quickly up into the air.

Meetings, meetings, meetings.

I tear myself away to discuss the possible arrangements that will give the world our machine on terms that we believe are fair. Father warned us to be on guard. I will not be so foolish as to sign an unfavourable agreement.

The British say that they are interested, but that the patent controversy puts our claims in jeopardy. The Germans say that they would like to buy our flying machine, but want assurance that we have legal claim to our invention.

Wiping oil off the floor of the shop with a newspaper. Pausing for a moment when an article catches my eye.
"Santos-Dumont has won the Archdeacon Cup with a flight of two hundred and twenty metres in his flying machine."

The others are copying our results, but they do not understand how we have arrived at our conclusions. In order to unlock the secrets of human flight, we had to find a way to test two-hundred-summers-worth of wings in a matter of weeks.
Our rivals test one set of wings at a time.
There is no one who seems to realize, including Octave Chanute, that our great accomplishment has not been the building and flying of the world's first flying machine. It is the invention of a whole new method of procedure. In pursuit of the secret of flight, we have been forced to invent the science of aeronautics.

A stack of newspapers on the table at the shop. A pronouncement, of his intentions, by Octave Chanute.
"Since the Army specifications are so obviously modelled on the feats that the Wright Brothers claim that their flying machine is capable of, I no longer feel that I should consider myself as bound to maintain the promise of secrecy that I once gave to them. The Wrights have gone public and so will I. I will publish the Wright specifications as I understand them."

A grove of trees ahead. I am too high to land and too low to go over their tops. I turn to the left – a very short radius. A quick turn and then I circle back towards the grandstand. The members of the crowd who are standing on the ground are running this way, and looking up and pointing, as though they can't believe the proof of their eyes.

"Are you aware, Monsieur Wright, of how far ahead of other inventors your first flight has put you?"
"Did you realize that your machine could do so many amazing things?"
"Do you realize that no one expected you to fly, let alone perform the miracles that you have performed for us today?"

I can feel the noise of the crowd below. I can feel their outpouring of excitement. It is the quickness of the launching and the sharpness of the turns that have startled them. This is flying, not the impotent flapping of the earth-bound, wing-clipped barnyard birds that they are used to. Hats are waving. Arms are flailing. People in the grandstand are standing up. People are cupping their hands and shouting invisible words. Two old men are exchanging hugs. I'm sure they never thought they would see the day. They have never witnessed anything like this. All previous flights have been crude hops. I know that no one in France has seen turns like this before.

Icarus dumped a pile of feathers on the sand. His feet were warm, but not burnt. As he gathered the feathers, he had run from shade to shade.

"Many types of birds can fly; many types of fish can swim," said Daedalus, who was bending over the fire. "If we can build wings from the natural elements that surround us here, my son, and these wings allow Man to fly, then who can say that flying is not as natural for Man as for the birds?"

Two circles around the field. I could go on longer, but I feel the need of a pause. I want to get a sense of the thoughts of the crowd below me. Three-quarters of a circle in a radius of about thirty yards, then I dip down and skid along the grass in front of the grandstand. It is important to me that I land with my wings held level.

Meetings, meetings, meetings.
I tear myself away, and leave the Flyer in the shed, to meet with those who wish to gain control of our creation.
Captain Ferber writes in L'Aérophile that none of our patents is worth anything. He says that our patents are invalid because our ideas were common knowledge in 1902. As proof, he cites the speeches of Octave Chanute.
The English say that they will monitor the situation. The Germans say that they will wait and see.

Daedalus placed a few more twigs under the fire and continued to stir the pot of wax.
"The design of the wings is of the utmost importance, my son. The question is not so much of the mood of the gods, but of the behaviour of matter in relation to the qualities of Man. By what framework will Man extend himself? At what point does a bunch of twigs, a length of fishing net, a pile of feathers and a pot of wax become a wing that will carry a human cargo through the air? The question is very simple: how many feathers will allow a man to fly?"

Great cheers and a standing ovation. People are hugging one another and waving their hats. They are shouting, but I can barely hear them. The motor is buzzing, the chains are clacking. I move the lever and shut things off. The crowd is not very large and yet the volume of sound is momentous. It is a pleasure after all that has gone so wrong. This is turning out to be an excellent day. I am pleased that everything has gone so well so far.

I wish that I was at home.
Or better yet, I wish that the others could be here, today, with me. I am sure that Katharine would be thrilled to see the crowds. She would be pleased, as well, to see how I am dressed. She is always admonishing me to take care to dress the part. Collar, coat and tie. "There might be photographs," she says. "You must always dress the part if you are to believe in yourself. You and Orville are not 'rude mechanicals'; you are inventors."

"Could we have an interview, Monsieur Wright?"
"Will the flying machine be for sale?"
"Could we have a photograph of you standing beside your machine?"

I have told them that I will go up for a second flight. Moving the machine over to the catapult, attaching her and signalling the men to start. The front rudder has been working very well. I think the measurements are just about right. Fourteen and a half inches from the front, for the hinge, is just about perfect. It is new and I am learning, but with a little more practice I am sure I will have complete control.

Readying the machine. A tangled rope in the catapult that needs attending. A person among the spectators waves a newspaper. I pause politely while he reads me what it says.

"Henri Farman has won the Deutsch-Archdeacon Prize for a close-circuit flight of one kilometre. There is no doubt that Messieurs Farman and Delagrange, who are visiting the capitals of Europe to demonstrate their flying machine, will soon be able to make the claim that they have flown a distance of fifty kilometres or more."

When I compare the machines that the French have flown, I can easily see that despite their knowledge of "Le Système Wright", they are still at least five years away from matching our accomplishment. Trial and error takes many years. They have no idea of the procedures that we were forced to devise.

If the crowd could only know as they shout their congratulations – "Bravo! Il vole! Il Vole!" – that I am once again learning how to operate a new flying machine, they would probably be very surprised. I am sure that it looks quite easy from the ground. The levers are difficult to operate without mistakes. It will take a while to master the give and take of the control mechanisms. The winds here are gusty and I must constantly adjust the machine when I am buffeted, but I can easily make turns of three hundred feet. I am reining in the speed until I learn the machine.

"Why have you been so secretive, Monsieur Wright?"
"Do you realize what you have accomplished today?"
"Why have you not unveiled your wonderful machine until now?"

Icarus stood on the edge of the precipice and flapped his wings up and down while he waited for his father to get himself ready. His muscles warmed up as he waved his arms in the breeze.

After a number of awkward gestures, his father tied the sandal-laces that lashed the wings to his body by holding them with one hand and pulling the laces tight with his teeth.

Once more the catapult lets go and I spring up for a second flight. This time, I will show them a figure-eight. No French aviator has ever done this. Their machines are barely able to turn. They haven't figured out the mechanism that will allow them to bank as they make a turn. They lumber around on a flat plane, like a farm-wagon, lurching in the air. To dip the wings and lean into a turn has never occurred to them.

I wish that Orville could be here to hear the cheering. He would love to see the arms waving and the looks on people's faces as I swoop in low and then climb back up again.

Neither Orville nor I should ever be alone. We never should have agreed to separate.

I wish the family could be here as well.

If only Father and Lorin and Netta and the children could be here. Above all, I wish that Orville could be here to see what, together, we have accomplished. We have successfully demonstrated, before the crowds of Europe, the world's first practical heavier-than-air, powered, human-piloted, controlled flying machine.

The crowds have wondered why I don't smile. The pain of my blisters has been intense, the work of restoration of the damaged Flyer has been gruelling, the awkwardness of helpers whose understanding of technical terms is a double-language away, but I think that the main reason that I don't smile is that I miss what I have always had at home.

To have success is very nice, but I know that if I were home, and the events of this day were ours to celebrate, we would all walk back to 7 Hawthorne Street, and shut the door on the badgering newspapermen, and the curious crowds, and the endless questions, and rustle up one of those delicious, endless, Wright-family-celebratory meals.

An article, in the Miteilungen, by Octave Chanute. I ask around for someone who speaks German. One of the workers translates it to me as best he can.

"The Wrights have made a mistake. They have spent years in negotiations that have borne no fruit. The cause is the price of their machine, which a person in my position must see as ridiculous. The Wrights have bargained and they have lost. Anyone in the field of aeronautics can see that the airship – the powered balloon – will be of more use in the event of war. The Wright Flyer, as interesting as it is, has been greatly overestimated in the impact that it will have. Truth to tell, in peacetime or in war, the Wright Flyer will have very limited use. The Wrights had better lower their price and make a sale."

"I do not believe the gods are jealous of Man," Daedalus said, as he slowly waved his arms to warm them up. "The only creature that is jealous of Man is another man. The gods have often rewarded audacity, as I have said. But one thing they always punish is human stupidity. I have stayed alive and relatively healthy, my son, because I never let my desires outpace my abilities. No human has ever flown in the air before. We do not know what we will find. We must maintain a moderate height. If we fly together, we will succeed. Now promise me, my son, that you will stay within the range that is logical for a human to pursue."

"Yes, Father," said Icarus, as he moved his wings up and down. "I promise that I will respect the limits of Man."

"Are you aware, Monsieur Wright, that today you have made history here in France?"

I climb a little higher, to avoid the tops of the trees, and prepare for a turn. We knew we were way ahead and now we have proven it. We were twenty years ahead until they caught on to "Le Système Wright", with their lumbering, crude contraptions. Well, now they are seeing what "Le Système Wright" can actually do. I bank around and then straighten my line. I head back towards the grandstand. Hats are waved and thrown in the air. I swoop above a cheering crowd of waving arms.

Chapter 9
Orville Wright 3

Fort Myer, Virginia
September 3 1908

A good day at Fort Myer.
The winds are from the north-west. About three miles per hour. 4:37 p.m. I don't think that conditions will ever get much better, but I am not quite ready to make an official demonstration of our wares. I don't know why there is a small crowd gathered. I never told anyone that this would be one of the official trials. There are one or two things that I want to check before I will officially fly.

The great god Apollo leaned forward from his throne. "Surely I have misheard you, my son," he said to Phaeton. "I thought I heard you say that you wanted to drive the Chariot of the Sun." Apollo smiled but didn't laugh, and a few of the others smiled as if they were sick.
"Yes, Father. That is exactly what I want."
"Perhaps I spoke too hastily when I made those promises to your mother," Apollo said. "I should have stopped at the blue rose-bush that I created for her, and not made any promises for the unborn child."

Great news from France. Great news of Wilbur's success.
He has demonstrated the practical nature of human flight for all of Europe to see. He has begun a new era in the life of human-kind.
He has been given a few inches of space in the Washington newspapers.

"What is it that your brother has accomplished in France, Mr. Wright?"
"Is it a balloon or a flying machine that he has flown?"
"Do you think that the French are easily impressed, Mr. Wright?"

A grim crowd and a small one. They are standing around and chatting in small groups. Perhaps the baseball game or the latest military gossip. Putting in time while someone fiddles with a contraption that no one in the Army has taken seriously. What was the name again – Orville Wright or Orville Wrong? Waiting until it's an appropriate time to leave. Wanting to be here just long enough to be able to say that they gave the thing a chance. That they knew all along that the strange contraption would never leave the ground. None of them seems to expect to be a witness to the birth of practical human flight.

And why has Glenn Curtiss been given permission to watch me as I prepare? He is one of our competitors. He should never have been allowed to watch me work.

"I cannot change my mind," said Phaeton. "Mother taught me not to lie, and if I change what I have said, it would make what I have said seem like an untruth."

"What did he say?" asked Apollo of the old men standing next to him.

"It is very hard to tell," said Old Man Winter. "I assume that he will hold you to your word." Old Winter leaned over as he spoke and Phaeton moved a little further away.

Apollo looked very grave and shook his head. "That is the only wish that I would be sorry to have to grant."

It is wonderful at the Cosmo Club. A view of Washington from the window, and satin pillow-cases on the bed. After the sand and the cold of Kitty Hawk, the luxury is welcome.

But sleepless nights are sleepless nights. Satin pillow-cases or sand-filled blankets, I regret the loss of sleep. My nights are filled with the turbulence of disturbing dreams. Greek gods and broken flying machines; runaway chariots and sputtering engines. How can a nightmare occur without a wink of sleep?

I can only hope with the news from France that things will change.

The news from France has been wonderful, but no one reads the foreign news here. If it hasn't happened in Washington or New York, it hasn't happened, it would seem. The news reports of Wilbur's flight are looked upon as those of the French aviators have been: too far away and too unlikely to be credited as legitimate news.

The feats of carnival performers are given very little space in the Washington newspapers.

I worry about Wilbur being alone.

I assume that he is recuperated from the accident in which he burnt his arm, but I know that Wilbur would never tell me if he was in pain. If he was here, or I was there, I could see what he was like, and I could ease the burden of facing so many pressures on his own.

Well, I could have told them it would be a waste of time to come today. There will be nothing spectacular today, if I have my way. Nothing except a very limited test. All I want to do is to find out what needs to be changed before I attempt to meet all of the terms of the Army contract. And I will not rush things until I am good and ready. I will not hurry no matter how many people I appear to disappoint.

"Are you aware of the claims of your competitors, Mr. Wright?"
"Do you put any credibility in their claims of-heavier-than-air flight?"
"Do you feel that Glenn Curtiss is your closest aeronautical competitor?"

Glenn Curtiss is our nemesis. We are constantly under attack. The competition is using our own methods to compete with us.

He entered our bicycle shop as a fellow aviation enthusiast, full of reassurances that he had no intention of violating the legal protection of our patents. We assumed that his honesty, and the law's protection, would see us through.

We were foolish to relax, for an hour, and let down our guard.

I miss the family back at home.

Home is only half-listening to Katharine as she talks about the flights of the antique Greeks, wanting to listen to her stories, but also wanting to continue our discussion about lift and centre of pressure and degree of turn.

Prometheus and Leonardo; Icarus and Daedalus; Phaeton and Apollo. The list goes on and on.

Her stories are wonderful, but we are so caught up in our own world – of data, technical terms, numbers and equations – that we are almost relieved when she turns back to her lessons and lets us proceed.

The parade ground is very small. Seven hundred by one thousand feet barely gives me enough room to get off the ground, let alone to fly. I will no sooner get into the air than I must make a turn. I couldn't convince anyone in the Army that their convenience was not the most important factor in the decision as to where I should attempt to fly. We have never made a flight over such a postage-stamp-sized field before.

Sitting in my room in the Cosmo Club in Washington. The evening lights in the city are a sight for tired eyes. Turning reluctantly from the view and looking through the mass of reading that I must do.

A comment, in L' Aéronautics, by Octave Chanute.

"The sureness with which the Wrights proceeded towards their successes has only been matched by the colossal blunder of their conduct since. Bringing lawsuits at this time, when the flying machine is being developed, will slow down the steady advance of aerial design. It will antagonize other inventors, who want nothing more than to get on with their work, and will cause many of them to launch a search into the history of patents. It is only fair to warn the Wrights that a search of the history of patents might well prove they are erroneous in many of their most important claims."

Satin sheets and sweat-soaked pillows at the Cosmo Club. Sleepless nights and painful dreams in which ten years of amazing accomplishments appear to be slowly and very surely slipping away.

The members of the press play cards in the drill-shed at Fort Myer. They wonder when I will finish tinkering and attempt to fly. They are interested in the race to demonstrate a practical flying machine. They ask my comments on any articles that they happen to read.

An article in the magazine, Aeronautics, by Glenn Curtiss, discusses the art of the movable-wing, as developed for his new machine, The White Wing. The article fails to state that the main features of the machine have been derived from the Wright patent of 1906.

My first test-flight in the new machine. There has been no time to test it for what I am sure will be problems. I haven't flown for a very long time. No one can suspect how precarious the demonstration of the Flyer is. The Army's ignorance of the difficulties demands that I perform miracles on top of miracles. They are expecting the miracle of flight; I am hoping for the double-miracle of a flight over a postage-stamp-sized field.

Apollo leaned down from his throne. His eyes were piercing and Phaeton could barely see his father through squinting eyes.

"Please withdraw the request that you have made," the Sun God asked. "You are merely a mortal, and yet you ask what no mortal should be so foolish as to even have the notion to consider."

There was no laughter now. Every face around the throne looked very grave.

"Even the gods would never transgress upon my prerogative. No god but me has ever driven the Chariot of the Sun. Are you sure that you will not withdraw your request?"

For a moment, Phaeton thought of making his request a drink of water. He hadn't had a drink since he'd left his home. The gods would all laugh and his father would grin with relief and order it to be done. He swallowed the dryness in his throat and spoke these words: "But I promised another boy that I would drive the Chariot of the Sun. I could never return to school if I change my mind. My mother told me that you would grant me whatever I should wish."

The soldiers pull the weight up on the catapult. A signal from me that I am ready, and they let it go. Down the track and off the ground. It is always surprising to me how quickly I am sprung up into the air. There must be a few in the crowd who are impressed at how quickly it has happened. Especially after days of waiting around with nothing to see. However, I am not here today to entertain. Keeping the speed down and flying low to the ground. Better to take it easy and be error-free than to provide a spectacle and lose control.

"You will not change your mind?" asked Apollo.

The voice boomed off the walls. Phaeton swallowed again and cleared his throat and then he spoke: "No father, I cannot. I promised my best friend at school. I said that I would drive the Chariot of the Sun. I will be careful as can be. I would only want to drive it for just one day."

One and a half times around the drill grounds. About thirty-five feet off the ground. About thirty-six miles per hour. Well, at least I have their attention. At least some of the groups have paused long enough to look. Well, I am sorry to disappoint them, but I am going to land. I could go on, but I have noticed some things that need to be taken care of. Better to land and to make some adjustments before I am ready to make my attempt at a serious run.

"Would it not be better to pool your ideas with other competitors, Mr. Wright?"
"Is that not what Mr. Chanute has called on you to do?"
"Is it not true that the secrets of flight are in the public domain?"

In September 1906, Glenn Curtiss visited us in Dayton. It was a very friendly visit from a fellow enthusiast. We were guarded, but we were also pleasant hosts. We invited him to the bicycle shop and showed him our propeller designs and let him have a peek at the Flyer photographs. He was very pleasant and gracious as he asked his many questions. He thanked us and reassured us as he left.

Now we wish that we had warned him to stay away.

I miss the family back at home.

Home is Father, spilling the teaspoonful of sugar into his tea-cup and telling us that if you walk a mile away from 7 Hawthorne Street you can feel the level of trust going down; ride the train a hundred miles from 7 Hawthorne Street and you'd better assume that you are travelling in hostile territory.

Our experiences since Kitty Hawk have been of a kind that have underlined his words.

Skidding along on the grass. The crowd breaks ranks and runs toward me. I think I have made an impression after all. Bumping along the ground as the crowd converges. Perhaps I have won a few military sceptics even with such a small flight. Wait until they see just what the Wright Flyer can actually do.

Sitting in the reading-room of the Cosmo Club. There is every newspaper in the world for one's reading pleasure. The members are very kind. They draw my attention to any comments which have been made about the Wrights.

A comment by Octave Chanute.

"It can be said, with truth, that almost all inventors profit legitimately from the ideas and the endeavours of their predecessors. As far as the Wright achievement goes, I would like to put on record that it was Wenham who proposed the bi-plane glider. For my part, I added a reinforced frame and published my design in my book, Progress in Flying Machines. It was at this point that the Wrights approached me for assistance. Truth be told, I believe that the chief Wright innovation is in the addition of a motor to the basic configuration of the glider. It is this which has made the Wrights stand out from the crowd."

Glancing around and assessing the landing. The right-hand side of the front skid seems to have broken. The main brace and a short brace both seem to have snapped as well. A skid wire is pulled out of its hinges, and a bolt is sheared. The water-pipe hose has worked her way loose. I'll have to look her over carefully and make my repairs.

"Why, Mr. Wright, if you have patented your ideas, do you claim that others are using your system to fly?"

"Have the courts not been enough to protect your ideas?"

"What is your proof that Mr. Curtiss has not discovered his innovations on his own?"

Glenn Curtiss's designs are a direct steal from the inventions of the Wright Flyer.

He wrote to us and asked us questions – about centre of pressure and camber and the way in which the fabric of the wings should be applied – and we answered him and directed his attention to our patents.

He assured us that he would respect our legal rights.
We feel as if a burglar has entered our home.

A glance at the watch as everyone comes running towards the machine. Time in the air was about one minute, eleven seconds. Mostly soldiers running towards me. None of the Army brass seems to be impressed, but that's to be expected. The contract demands a lot more from the Flyer than this. Well, they will have to be impressed when I make my adjustments. Soon, they'll see just exactly what the Flyer can do.

Phaeton stood beside his father. The two of them stood beside the Chariot of the Sun. The Horses of the Sun pranced and snorted and pawed the ground. The chariot was mostly made of gold, but Phaeton noticed that the axle and the spokes were made of silver, and the seat was made of chrysolites and diamonds. So that was why the sun was so very bright.

"Even Zeus, who hurls the thunderbolts, has never asked to drive the Chariot of the Sun," said Apollo. He took the rays off his head, and placed them on the head of his son. The rays were wobbly and he had to adjust the fit.

"Stay on the middle course," the father said, as he adjusted the strap that held the rays. "Mid-way between the northern and the southern zones. If you go too high, you will burn the dwellings of the gods. If you go too low, you will set the earth on fire. You will see the tracks in the clouds. All you have to do is follow where I have gone so many times before. Do not go striking out on your own to unknown territory, my son. The middle way is the safest way to go."

"Oh I promise, Father. We are taught to be honest at our school. I would never, ever go back on my given word."

I worry about Wilbur facing so many pressures alone.

I am convinced that when the hose came loose and sprayed Wilbur with burning water it was due to the fact that he had been distracted by the same things that cry out for my attention. The pressure of working on the flying machine, writing to the aeronautical journals, answering questions from the newspaper men, talking to the crowds of curious onlookers and worrying over the lack of a buyer for our invention is very draining.

Neither Wilbur nor I should ever work alone. We never should have agreed to work alone.

I miss the family back at home.

Home is Lorin and Netta and the children – Milton and Ivonette and Leontine and Horace – coming over for a Sunday afternoon, after a morning at church, and asking Uncle Will and Uncle Orv if they can have one more show in the parlour with their two favourite actors – Sam Bonebrake and Jim Higgenbotham.

It is the Sabbath after all. Father hesitates before he tells us that perhaps it would be better if we draw the blinds.

About twelve minutes after six. The soldiers are running towards me. Hard to tell whether they are impressed. Need more screws at the top of the radiator. The radiator seemed to jump back during the jar of the landing. Better get her back to the shed and start to make my repairs.

Apollo held his son's hand as they both stepped up into the chariot. He placed the reins in Phaeton's hands, and gave him some hints on how to steer, and stepped down and backed away among the other gods on the platform. Then he nodded and Dawn threw open the purple doors that led to the East.

Phoebus clucked the horses, but none of them made a move. Then he turned towards his father, but before he was able to ask his father if he looked like a sun god the horses plunged ahead, and the reins were jerked like a noose that closed on his hands.

The Chariot of the Sun was fully launched.

"Could you do it again for the card-players who were in the drill shed, Mr. Wright?"

Very soon, I should be ready to shake the dust off the wings and fly my route. A few solo flights and then I'll be ready for a passenger. Perhaps I'll ask Lieutenant Lahm. He said he would like to go. Though Lieutenant Falois, at one hundred and thirty pounds, seems made for the task. The Army insists that the Flyer must carry a pilot and an observer. One of the requirements is to take a passenger along for the ride.

Chapter 10
The Wright Brothers 4

Kitty Hawk, North Carolina
December 17, 1903

A cold day at Kitty Hawk.
The two of us together. Apart from the others. Trading the bowler for a cap. Make it stay where it's supposed to with a safety pin. Shaking hands. "Remember, ten or fifteen feet – that's the optimum." "We'll keep her just the perfect height above the sand" "Not too high and not too low." "High enough to fly and low enough to handle a crash."

Prometheus crouched behind a rock and studied the fire. It danced in the stone circle in the courtyard. It was interesting to watch it. He had noticed how the flames would die down low for a while and then would be fanned alive by the quickening breeze.
He had been hiding now for hours outside of Zeus's palace on Mount Olympus while an angry debate was raging among the gods. From where he crouched, he could see into the palace – past the flames of the fire, towards Zeus's golden throne and the great stone circle that comprised the seats of all of the gods.
They had been debating since he had arrived – something was definitely causing anger – though nothing so important as to keep them away from the wine. In twos and threes, they would separate themselves and stroll out onto the courtyard of the palace for a sip or two of wine and a breath of fresh air.
Now Hera and Athena, whispering stealthily. Now Hades and Poseidon, speaking angrily of Zeus. He had been forced to hide behind an outcrop, waiting for a time when there would be no gods in the courtyard in front of the palace.

Well who would have thought that this would be the case? All along, we have felt that the others were approaching the invention of the flying machine all wrong. We thought that the others were wrong to build their machines with massive motors and thoughtless wings, and then to fling them into the air and hope for the best.

The water we swim in; the air that we breathe. A cloud of numbers we take into our lungs and into our bloodstream. The tools that we have around the bicycle shop – hammer, file, tin shears, soldering iron – making a practical and working flying machine. The hands-on application of our emerging understanding of the age-old forces of nature.

The internal combustion engine - weight-to-horsepower - eight horsepower - twelve horsepower - fuel- pistons - horizontal cylinders - crankshaft - chains - propellers.

Kitty Hawk is bleak in mid-December.
Most of the birds have gone and only a few gulls patrol the shallows on the edges of the beach. There are nights when the shriek of the wind means we cannot sleep. Nights when we have to go outside and shore up the sheds in the midst of an Atlantic gale.
Kitty Hawk in mid-December makes us think, more and more, of the warmth of home.

Relaxing in the shed. A little leisure time. Reading about the rivalry once again. A shake and the newspaper empties its acres of sand.
"A failure of the launching system," Professor Langley explains to the reporters. "It was not the flying machine at all that was at fault in our first attempt. The launching device snagged. A most unfortunate occurrence. It reached out and curtailed the speeding missile's forward progress. If this unfortunate check had not happened, a new epoch would have been seen. Yes, I would call this trial successful. Yes, I would. Despite the minor setback, I declare this flying machine to be capable of human flight."

No time to regret things now. We were sorry to have to waive the trials. We had planned to test the Flyer without the motor. We were going to treat her as a glider. Get used to the way she handles. Make adjustments in her steering. Make sure that she will respond as we have planned. Everything we have developed for her is new. She is larger and heavier than any of our gliders have been. She has to be to lift the weight of the motor into the air. She has a number of new controls. We should have tested her for a month. But problems delayed our tests. Professor Langley just might be lucky. Winter weather is moving in. We decided to put the motor on and try her just as soon as she was ready to fly.

Leonardo leaned back on a rock. As much as possible, he had arranged the folds of his robe to cushion the seating and ease the burning feeling in his aching hip.
The air was clear and cool and the sun was warm.
What was it that would power a man through the air? Man could not become a bird, but until he could match a bird, he was not fully a man. Surely he was capable of doing everything that a bird could do.
He opened up his notebook and started to draw.

We have felt that we should start with gliding. Start with kite gliding – a kite big enough to have a man on board. The problem, as we saw it, was that man had never learned to fly, and so it was impossible to sort the errors in the design from the errors made by the operator while in flight.

We would learn to fly, in the air, we decided, by practising balance and quick response, as a bicycle rider learns to control a bicycle, and gradually we would learn control of the air.

1,200 rpm - 15.76 horsepower - 1,090 rpm - 11.81 horsepower - 12 horsepower available - drive-shaft - sprockets - 4" piston - 9.5 horsepower - weight of machine.

How nice it will be to spend Christmas Day at home.

Every year, despite his many travels, if at all possible, Father has made it a point to be home with the family on Christmas Day. We wish to do no less.

We have decided that, no matter what happens here, in December, at Kitty Hawk, we will strike camp and go home to Dayton for Christmas Day.

Talking to the five. "Don't look so sad." "Remember that we have never had a major accident." "Laugh and hallo and clap your hands and make a big cheer when we start." "Remember, we have to know when the machine has left the ground." "You can't always tell what's happening when you're at the controls." Have to get them to shout above the motor noise. "Let's send her off with a noisy welcome when she takes to the air."

We have learned to respond to the breeze. To react to the gusts of wind. To be ready for the buffets of the air currents, to lulls and eddies and up-draughts.

And we have built a glider that can fly. We have mastered the mysteries of lift, and the challenge of lateral control, and overcome the baffling surprise of reverse turning.

And all along, we have believed that when we had mastered control of the air, we could order a motor from a catalogue, and attach it to our machine and fly away.

How wrong we were to assume that kind of ease.

Seven hundred pounds - four horizontal cylinders - 201 cubic inches - bore and stroke - lathe and drill press - crankshaft - block of machine steel - 6 inches by 31 inches - five-eighths inches thick - hammer and chisel.

Home is 7 Hawthorne Street, Dayton Ohio.

This is where we grew up. Although the family has lived elsewhere, in the past, this is where, it seems, we have always lived. This is the place where we come home from the world to renew ourselves. This is the house we paint in the spring and the garden that we turn over in the fall. This is the house where we built the verandah – our host for long discussions on curvature and lift and resistance on cool summer evenings.

Katharine and Father sitting in the rocking chairs. We, sitting on the swing and discussing aeronautics far into the night by the light of the moon.

Slipping onto the bottom wing. Feet pressed against the board. Hands wrapping around the controls. Sliding side to side to test the hip cradle. Wing, warping wires and rudder. Both working together this time. Nice to have the padding. It'll be especially nice when we nudge ourselves into the ground. Thirty miles an hour as she bites into the sand. Left hand on the front elevator control. Elevator up and elevator down.

Working smoothly.

Leonardo chewed on a piece of bread. An interesting shadow fell across the rock and over his knee.

He put the piece of bread down beside the loaf and went back to working steadily. The pen moved across the page. The afternoon sun moved as steadily across the hills.

The wings would have to be manoeuvrable, that was certain. They would have to be able to duplicate the subtle adjustments of a bird in flight. And they would have to be large in span. They would have to be big enough to lift and carry the weight of a man.

Motors, motors, motors.

Ten letters to ten motor companies. All presenting specifications for a motor to be sent to Dayton, Ohio, to the Wright Cycle Company, in care of the Wright Brothers.

Brennan Motor Company, Buffalo Gasolene Motor Company, A. H. Funke Company, Daimler Manufacturing Company, Grant-Ferris Company, Mohler & DeGress Company, Motor Vehicle Power Company, E. R. Thomas Motor Company, Waltham Manufacturing Company, Winton Motor Carriage Company.

All we asked for was a motor which would meet a few simple requirements: we need a motor of no more than 180 pounds in weight and having at least eight or nine horsepower. That is all. A motor of that size and power would have a power-to-weight ratio that would lift and propel our machine.

How could we know that they all would turn us down? We thought that we could order a motor and bolt it into our flying machine. We thought that others were working on smaller and lighter motors.

19 pounds, finished and balanced - 180 pounds - 12 horsepower - 1,025 revolutions per minute - cast aluminum - cast iron pistons - piston rings - fuel system - one-gallon fuel tank - gravity feed.

Dayton is our brother, Lorin, and his wife, Netta, and their children, Milton, Ivonette, Leontine and Horace. Living two blocks away from our house on Hawthorne Street. When times get busy, Netta drops the children into the store and they watch us as we work on our bicycles. At home, we play games and make candy – caramel or fudge – with a thermometer that lets us know how long it should be boiled.

And we read to them – The Goop Tales: Alphabetically Told is their favourite book – and make magic lantern shows and produce theatrical spectaculars like the shadowgraph shows, with Sam Bonebrake and Jim Higgenbotham – two sheet metal characters whom we made for the children on a rainy afternoon in the bicycle shop.

Horizontal lever, in the centre. To the right, at one o'clock, the closed fuel line. To the centre, at twelve o'clock, the opening of the fuel cock, for the priming and starting of the engine. To the left, at eleven o'clock, the slipping of the tie-down line so we can start off down the track. Won't be long and we'll be doing exactly that.

All of the inventors have been so wrong. The massive motors that they have used to power their monstrosities have had no relation to a man and a pair of wings.

None of them has considered the problem of control. We know that a man cannot be shot through the air, as if he is sitting on an arrow; we know that a man must be in control of his machine, like a rider on a bicycle.

That is why we have solved the problem of lateral control, so the operator of the flying machine can right it in the buffets of the wind. That is why we have solved the problem of lift, so the wings will be the most efficient at lifting the man and the frame and the motor into the air. That is why we have solved the problem of side slip, so the man can steer the machine.

Now we have the flying machine but we have no motor. They have all been building motors that are large enough to power an automobile, but not small enough to propel a man and a flying machine. Now we find that none has considered the relation of power to weight. Others have strapped large motors onto wings and blasted them into the air, but none has considered the science of a motor that could actually contribute to the right balance of elements to fly.

We have moved so far ahead that we are alone. If we want a motor to power our machine, we will have to design and build one by ourselves.

Tube to the engine - hot water jacket- fuel valve - camshaft timing - chamber in the manifold - vaporization of the mixture - low-tension ignition - spark breaker arms - exhaust valves - intake valves.

Prometheus crouched behind the rock. Waiting, waiting, waiting. Inside, the debate raged on. Outside, as the day wore on, the gods conferred or idled aimlessly.

Once it was Zeus with a message for Iris to take to Hephaestus. The great, self-important Zeus. He of the large girth and fierce eyes. The self-decider of Man's limitations. The self-deluder, if he thought that Man would never acquire the possession of fire. Even Zeus didn't realize how limitless were the limits of Man.

It got very interesting when someone, a lesser god, of course, would take a stick and lean over and poke at some of the embers. Once, one of the minor gods – ordered to do so by Ares – came and gathered up an armload of wood and dumped it onto the fire. He came so close that Prometheus could feel his grunting breath.

Dayton is Charlie Taylor, who works for us in the bicycle shop. Who builds to our specifications and watches the shop while we are away at Kitty Hawk. It is Charlie's job and he does it well, as we expect him to – patching a bicycle tire for a customer or contributing to the making of the world's first flying machine.

It has all worked very well. To make the motor, we drew diagrams and Charlie pinned the paper above the work bench and set to work.

December moving onward. The temperature dropping down. Will there be time, Professor Langley, the newspaper reporters ask, for one more attempt to get your flying machine to fly?

"Yes, winter is coming on," Professor Langley answers. "No, my back is not to the wall. No, not at all. Yes, many people have lost their faith in the great experiment. Yes, some are saying that it is wrong of me to pursue this ages-old dream. But these nay-sayers will soon be proven wrong. Mankind has always been destined to fly, like the birds of the air. Millions of birds fly at their ease every day. Trial and error will be our watchword. Each attempt is a movement ahead. It is a matter of divining the secrets that are temporarily locked in the sky."

Another evening in the shed. All of us wrapped in blankets, after the dishes have been cleared away, leaning like old women towards the stove. Us on one side, and Octave Chanute on the other. His hands tucked under his elbows. Stamping his feet on the sandy floor before he speaks.

"Professor Langley might well be finished, you know. The waves of public ridicule, if he fails, are bound to take their toll. It would be an embarrassment for the Army. The Board of Ordinance and Fortification gave Professor Langley fifty thousand dollars for a public demonstration of the possibility of human flight, and what would it look like if the professor were to fail? The Army would abandon the development of the flying machine, that's one thing we can know for sure. Those who have ridiculed Professor Langley would see to that. Without government financial assistance, the work of Professor Langley could not go on."

To make a motor small enough, and powerful enough, we will have to design and build the motor by ourselves. Charley Taylor, in our bicycle shop, will have to build it to our specifications.

Velocity? Thrust? Drag? Power? An eight-horsepower motor, with ninety pounds of thrust, a speed of twenty-three miles per hour, with four horizontal in-line cylinders, water-cooled, and weighing 170 pounds.

This should give us the power-to-weight ratio that we need.

Splash lubrication - weight of engine - weight of fuel - weight of operator - 20 lb. per hp. - free from vibration - valves - heavier springs - amount of gasoline consumed per hour - 670 revolutions per minute.

Home is sponsoring local bicycle races, in order to advertise the Wright Cycle Company, and organising excursions into the country-side for all-day bicycle rides. Or checking the air in the tires for Katharine and Agnes Osborn and Margaret Goodwin and all of their cycling friends as they set out on a female excursion of their own.

Home is Ed Ellis and Jess Gilbert and Glen Osborn. Chess on the parlour table and canoe rides on the old canal. Home is fishing and hunting and a campfire and the sound of a mandolin and a harmonica drifting out over the water of the lake.

Leonardo paused. He remembered the bread, waiting beside him on the rock. I should eat. I should have something to eat.

Marks on a page. The lines of his thoughts. An attempt to capture something that he believed it was possible to capture.

It is very difficult, though. An attempt to draw something that no man has ever seen. A means of imagining the highest pitch that a man could possibly reach. Of arriving there before him and drawing the imaginary means of his arrival.

He brushed the crumbs away from his beard. There was a dryness in his throat. He had no wine to drink today. It was unfortunate that wine was too heavy for an aging fellow to carry.

A man would crouch inside this machine. He would place his feet just so, and his hands just so, and when he was ready, he would nod to the others who were helping him, and they would pull their hands away and release the machine.

A glance at the three instruments. The Richard hand anemometer. On the front centre strut, just to the right. An eight-bladed fan that rotates and turns the shaft that records the metres travelled. The long needle is the distance in metres. The short needle is the distance in units of ten metres each. Making sure that everything is ready for our flight.

Home is the two of us, on our bicycles, riding out to the Pinnacles on a Sunday afternoon so we can bird-watch. Spreading a blanket out on the grass and lying on our backs and looking for hours through the binoculars at the birds, while dipping, every so often, into the picnic basket.

Watching the pigeons and the buzzards – "Did that bird just drop a wing? Is he shifting his body-weight or is he just flicking the tiniest tip at the end of his wing?" – and dreaming what many people have assumed to be impossible.

Kitty Hawk is where we will fly, but Dayton is our home. Home is the strength that has sustained us.

The shed was cold. You could see your breath. Octave Chanute shivered and shuffled his feet. He pulled his blanket tighter around his neck, and leaned a little closer to the stove.

"I don't want the two of you to be disheartened by the prospect of another Langley failure," he said, "if it should come to that. Human flight might be further away in the future than any one might think, but, for my part, I want to cheer you on. It's best to avoid highs and lows. It is easy to become elated at the prospect of human flight, and then to become over-deflated when you realize that things have gone wrong. I have seen it with my gliders. I have been through the cycle of high hopes and bitter disappointments many times."

Then he stood up, and shivered and stamped and waited, while we moved his chair a little closer to the fire.

"Yes, the machine will be rebuilt," Professor Langley keeps insisting to the reporters. "The Great Aerodrome will be launched again. Yes, soon, if all goes according to schedule. Yes, I realize that we are well into December, but I have every confidence that there will be another attempt to fly the Langley Aerodrome by the end of the year."

But has the public not lost faith, Professor Langley?

"It is a certainty that man will learn to fly. It is embedded in the narratives of the old Greek storytellers. It is etched into the drawings of Leonardo. There is no doubt that someday humankind will learn to fly."

The professor leans forward, to make sure that every reporter is writing it down.

As the afternoon wore on, Prometheus waited. He knew what he would do if he had his chance. All he needed was a very brief time to snatch a piece of wood from the fire. He could run with this down the mountain. It looked as if the fire was attached to the wood.

Finally, the time came when the gods had exhausted their blustering. When even Zeus – huge, self-important Zeus – had yawned and mumbled that the assembly would be adjourned.

The afternoon grew drowsy. As soon as all were safely asleep, Prometheus crept across the courtyard, crouched low beside the fire, blew softly on the embers, admired the glow that pulsed in the charcoal, selected a tree branch with a tiny flame that looked promising, reached out his hand towards the fire, hesitated for a moment, looked over his shoulder – just a glance – then closed his fist around the branch and filched the precious secret of the gods.

Gravity-fed with gasoline. A quart and a half capacity. A drip system to vaporize the fuel. Twelve horsepower when done; four more than the needed eight. Enough to carry the extra number of pounds.

If our calculations are correct, this is the motor which will power our machine.

"There is a monster called Chimaera," Katharine says. "It is composed of all of the evils that seem to surround us. It gathers these forces in with the thirst of a sponge. Sheer havoc is its only discernable goal."

She is sipping tea as we all take a break in our evening reading. The sugar bowl draws Father away from his accounts.

"The boy is nervous and afraid, but he sharpens his spear and he bites his lip and he flexes his knees in the flanks of Pegasus and the monster rears on his haunches as the flying horse and rider attack from the air."

The stopwatch. The distance and the time will give us the speed. The Veedor engine revolution recorder, at the base of the engine crankshaft, will give us the engine and propeller turns. That will also help tell us the distance travelled in the air. The shut-off lever, for cutting the life to all of the instruments. When we touch the ground, we'll immediately shut off the switch, so all of our numbers will be accurate. Everything seems to be ready for our flight.

Chapter 11
Wilbur Wright 4

Le Mans, France
September 18, 1908

A perfect day in France.
Friday morning, eight o'clock. A perfect-weather day. Clear skies, a lifting breeze. Truly a day in a thousand. Today, I intend to win the Michelin and Commission d'Aviation prizes. I intend to set a record for the longest time in the air.

Icarus soared above the promontory where he had launched himself from the island. His father, Daedalus, soared with him. He circled his father in an up-draught, practising the flicking of the wing-tips that his father had told him about. It was the way that they retrieved their balance from the buffeting winds. Down below, the waves wrinkled as they made their way into shore.
We are the first human beings to fly, Icarus thought. Only those who have climbed high mountains have seen what we can see. He felt the breeze caress his cheek. He felt that Man had certainly been born to learn to fly.
Then his father left the up-draught and moved out over the sea and Icarus followed. There was enough of a breeze that he was able to soar with just an occasional movement of the arms. His father had told him to conserve his energy as much as he could.

There is a difference between the night and the day. During the day, there are successful flights and cheering crowds and flattering newspaper headlines. During the night, there are nightmares of malfunctions of the machine and of the possibility of crippling accidents and of business deals gone wrong, and always the hollow experience of having to work alone.
I know that for Orville it must be exactly the same.

Rolling the Flyer out of the shed. Watching every aspect of the move. "Allons! Allons, mes Amis!" The language is a barrier. These fellows don't realize how delicate the operation is. "Très gentile, s'il vous plait!" She must be handled gently. Every item on the machine is a compromise of weight and strength. One bump can cost a cancelled day of flight.

The response to the flights has been overwhelming. Newspapers are proclaiming a new age of man; people are astounded that man has been given wings; thousands from all over Europe have left their homes and are travelling to France to see the new phenomenon; honours are being offered; speeches are being made.

I am asked my opinion on art, literature, politics and even medicine. Newspaper reporters, millionaires and even kings are asking for permission to help to haul the weight to the top of the catapult. Everyone wants to take part in the wonder of the age.

We are hostages of the public imagination.

Letters arrive in bundles asking for help and advice and money. Songs are being written and our names are being mentioned as belonging in the company of famous men.

Little do they know that I live in constant fear of having an accident that will discredit all that Orville and I have accomplished or of not being able to repair the machine, should any mishap occur, due to the language barrier and the shortage of available parts.

"Can you tell us the secret, Monsieur Wright?"
"Why is it that you can fly so much better than anyone else?"
"What do you think of the European political situation?"

I worry about Orville being alone.

I wonder how he is holding up against the intensity of the scrutiny. The news of his flights is very good. He has caused a sensation that has eclipsed my acclaim in Europe. I only hope that he will not be too distracted. I hope that he will keep his mind on the details of every flight.

I wish that I were home.

At home, I would be sitting in the swing, on the verandah, while Father would be sitting in the rocking chair, after an exhausting session of checking and re-checking his church accounts.

We would be taking a break for tea – two teaspoonsful of sugar for Father – and Orville and I would have a few moments to chat about things. Whether the curve of the wing should be 1-in-12 or 1-in-22 or somewhere in between? We would argue for hours about the merits of the various wing-shapes.

Oh I wish I could be on the verandah – with Father and Katharine and Orville – for just five minutes out of one of the many, many evenings that I have spent alone here in France.

Father has said we'll stay close to the waves, Icarus thought, but I hope he will change his mind. I would love to soar up higher than imagination can possibly reach. To see what man has seen from hilltops is to make a mockery of flight. I wish to see what man has never seen.

Just then, he heard a zipping noise, and looked around to see what it was. His father was looking down, so he followed his gaze. There was a sailboat down below, and the zipping sound came again. King Minos's guards were exited and they were pointing up at the sky.

One guard was standing with his foot on the gunwale of the sailboat. He took an arrow from his quiver and placed it in his bow.

The newspapers pour in to Monsieur Bollée's shed. Stacks of them are placed upon the workbench. Everyone points out articles that they insist I take time to read. An interview, in The New York World, with Octave Chanute.

"I certainly do not believe, even for a moment, that the courts will support the Wright Brothers' claim that the basic principle which is the basis for the warping of wing-tips can possibly be patented. It is well-known, in aeronautical circles, that the fundamental principle that the Wright Brothers claim to have invented was well known to all who were involved in aviation well before the Wright Brothers ever entered into the field."

"Why has your family not accompanied you to Europe, Monsieur Wright?"
"Where is Octave Chanute, your spiritual father, to whom you owe so much of your success?"
"Do you think that air machines will one day be as common as horses?"

All of the boys are wearing the green cap that I brought over here from home. Now all the shops are selling "Le Chapeau Wright".

Every day, three thousand people stand outside Monsieur Bollée's shed and ask whether I am going to fly today. If weather or mechanical problems or fatigue makes the answer no, there is great deal more disappointment than I can bear.

A crowd of thousands. The roads were jammed before it was dawn. There are dozens of newspaper reporters. Everyone in France has come out to see me fly. A fellow could say it was a long, long way from Kitty Hawk. The French have been very gracious in their praise.

Offers, offers, offers.
The demonstration has had the desired effect. Offers to buy, rent, manufacture and sell our machine are pouring in from all over Europe. The road to Le Mans is jammed with traffic. Princes and millionaires are now as thick as fleas. Politicians and royalty are flocking to the scene. Many have asked to be taken aloft, but I have promised that one of the first will be Monsieur Bollée.

The English are eager to sign a deal. The Germans are urging me to scratch my name on the dotted line.

Now the problem is how to sift through the multitude of competing offers.

Reading the newspapers in the shed. Eating lunch with the French workers of Monsieur Bollée. Louis Blériot is asked what he thinks of the exploits of Wilbur Wright.

"I consider that for us in France, and everywhere, a new era of mechanical flight has commenced."

Our competitors have acknowledged our accomplishment. We have finally been given credit for what we have done.

The newspaper are filled with the exploits of Orville. What he has done is now putting me in the shade.

It seems that all of America has gone wild. All of Europe is talking about Orville and the wonderful things that he has done. The newspapers are filled with the details of all of his flights.

"How does it feel to be suddenly famous, Monsieur Wright?"
"Are you aware of the extent to which your celebrity has grown?"
"Do you feel that your flights have eclipsed the acclaim of Monsieur Chanute?"

The nightmares never cease.

Letters, articles, interviews. The voices of the newspaper reporters. The questions of the crowd. We had braced ourselves for success, but we never knew how relentless success can be.

Much better weather this week. A short flight almost every day. The crowds marvel each time I leave the ground and circle back and swoop above their heads. "Il vole! Il vole!" every time I take to the air. None of them seems to realize that the machines are still an experiment. The flying machine is being invented each time we fly.

I wish I were at home.

There was a day, at home, in the early days, when Octave Chanute – the inventor from Chicago; the world expert in aeronautics; the gracious elderly gentleman – came to our house for a visit and a meal. Father was there, at his most courtly, and Katharine, at her most charming, and we all sat and ate – a little too formal for chatter at first – and then we all moved out to the verandah, for after-dinner tea, and a wonderful, rollicking, laughter and wonder-filled discussion of the possibility of the dream of human flight.

It is dark here in the shed. I wish I were home, at 7 Hawthorne Street, on a night like tonight.

Readying the Flyer on the track. "S'il vous plait!" "S'il vous plait!" Gesturing for space. Asking the men to ask the crowd to please move back. It's not enough to just wait and watch as I prepare the machine. They seem to want to press in and be part of the experience too. They mean well, I know, but the crowds are becoming dangerous. One bump and I will have to postpone the flight while I take the time to check the whole machine. That has always been our rule. We haven't stayed alive by being careless.

Taking a moment to read the newspapers in the shed. A short break in a succession of ten-hour days. René Glasner, a balloonist, is asked to consider the accomplishment of the Wrights.

"Compared with the Wrights, we are as children."

Our competitors have acknowledged our accomplishment. We have finally been given credit for what we have done.

Offers, offers, offers.

The offers pour in from all over Europe. Everyone wants to enter the age of flight. The English say that they will build an airfield on the Isle of Sheppey. The Germans want me to sell the machine to them instead of to France.

The problem now is how to decide how best to proceed.

"Have you been reading of the flights of your brother, Monsieur Wright?"
"Of the two of you, which one deserves the most credit for your success?"
"Are you competing with your brother, Monsieur Wright?"

Things to watch for on this flight today.

Most of the flights have been short because of the over-heating of the motor. I hope that I have over-come the problem for today. The new system of levers has been much more difficult to get used to operating than I ever would have thought. Two minor accidents alone were due to the change in levers. I've had a week of practice. I think today I'll be all right. There are thousands here to watch today. I want to show them a degree of control that has never been seen.

Another arrow zipped past Icarus and Daedalus.

The guards have sighted us. Now we are going to die, thought Icarus.

Just then, Daedalus soared higher, and Icarus scrambled to follow. Daedalus looked down as Icarus rose after him. Icarus, too, caught an up-draught and rode it up into the sky.

Then Icarus tried to wave to his father, as a thank-you for taking them out of the range of the arrows, but he remembered that they couldn't communicate in this way. Their arms were strapped inside the gigantic wings. They could only speak to each other with their actions and their thoughts. He had followed his father's lead without signals at all.

Things to watch for on this flight today.

This machine has one-third more power than our machine of 1904-05, yet my speed is only about thirty-seven miles an hour. I wonder why the velocity is so low. The power of our engine is about twenty-eight horsepower. I can probably get thirty-one horsepower by advancing the spark. I will try it today and hope that it will work out.

Reading in the shed and sipping a coffee. A short break from tuning the engine. A pile of newspapers from all over Europe is stacked on the bench.

Léon Delagrange is asked what he thinks of the recent flights of Wilbur Wright.
"We are beaten! We just don't exist!"

Our competitors have acknowledged our accomplishment. We have finally been given credit for what we have done.

"Why do you not want photographs taken of your machine, Monsieur Wright?"
"Do you not have a patent on your invention?"
"Do you not wish to share your achievement with the world?"

Things to watch for on this flight today.

The tail on this machine is far too large. Five feet ten inches times twenty-four inches gives me much too large a surface for my turns. It is fine when I work it right, but if I move the tail the wrong way when I turn, the response is far too great, and makes it hard to correct. It sends me into a spin before I can recover from the mistake and get back on track.

Icarus looked down at the sea below and saw a glint as an arrow rose and made an arc and then fell aimlessly down and down and into the water. He felt safe up here at this altitude. The guards on the boat below seemed far away.

Icarus moved his wings very gently, with the subtlest of moves, and the apparatus responded. He looked down and the sailboat grew smaller and finally was gone.

The men are in place to pull the weight for the catapult. The crowds have settled back. Everything is about ready to begin. What is it that needs to be attended to? It is important that I check everything that the men have done to make sure that there have been no slips of attention. I have to concentrate on the things that I have to watch for. Neither one of us is used to crowds. I hope that Orville doesn't let the crowds become a distraction. Now to start the motor and we can begin.

"Are you aware, Monsieur Wright, that you are a hero?"
"Are you aware that boys are wearing an imitation of your cap?"
"Are you aware that you are recognizable all over the world?"

A stack of newspapers on the bench in Monsieur Bollée's shed. All over Europe, there is warmth. Those who stagger in short hops, or flounder, in ragged turns, are asked to give their thoughts on what they have seen at Le Mans.

"The figure-eight of Wilbur Wright is the most astonishing thing that man has beheld since the day that Adam awoke to see the sun."

Our competitors have acknowledged our accomplishment. We have finally been given credit for what we have done.

The sunlight glinted on the waves. The two of them, father and son, flew on and on. At this rate, they would make the coast by nightfall.

It was as if they weren't father and son. If Icarus was below his father, he felt like the son. But if he caught a draft and soared above, he felt like the father. Sure, his father had invented the wings, but he was the one who obviously knew best how to use them.

There is much in what my father says, Icarus thought, though he is old and much too conservative to ever go far. He is right about the gods, though. They have never punished pride. It is stupidity they condemn. It is the failure to use their gifts that they deplore. They have placed the secrets of the universe in their laps. They are waiting for us to claim them. They despise all those who are reluctant to come and partake. The gods expect us to learn all of their secrets. The earth and all that is in it are ours to explore.

Pushing and shoving. What is this? "On arrive! On arrive!" "Please let us through!" Some new men are jostling their way to the front of the crowd. "Monsieur Wright! Monsieur Wright! We have just arrived!" "Do you have a statement to make about your brother?" "Well yes, of course. His flights in America have created quite a sensation here in Europe. I assume that there is the same general acclamation back home. If you will excuse me now, I – " "No, no! The accident!" "Do you have any comment to make on your brother's accident?"

A letter from Octave Chanute. Amid the deluge of mail, I spy, in the stacks of letters on the table, a familiar name. Settling down on the stool in the shed, the Flyer at my elbow, snatching a moment from a busy schedule, to read.

"My congratulations on your magnificent success in France. You cannot know how I feel when I see the recognition which is now accorded you by all and sundry. I have no doubt that you will receive a fortune for your labours. I can only stand on the side-lines, with everyone else, and wonder at your progress. I hope that you will occasionally find time to send me the news of your latest triumph. I can only hope that you will still speak to me when you both become millionaires."

"Accident? What accident? What do you mean?" "Your brother has crashed in America!" "Your brother and a passenger!" "Both of them were injured!" Orville and a passenger! "How are they? What kind of accident? We have always had plenty of accidents! What kind of accident was it?" "Apparently the accident is very serious, but there are no details" "Do you have any details from America that you can add?"

Terrible things happen because we are alone.
When Orville and I are together, we check and check and check. We talk everything over and then we check again. Monsieur Bollée and the others are very helpful, as I am sure Orville has excellent help too, but I am sure that this would not have happened if I had been there.
Neither Orville nor I should ever work alone. We never should have agreed to separate.

I wish I was at home.
When Mother was sick, or Orville was ill, or even when Father caught a cold, we were all together in the house, walking on tip-toes, boiling broth, adjusting a shawl or a knee-warming blanket, building up the fire, or summoning the doctor for a consultation – together as a family until the danger had passed.
Father and Katharine and Lorin are in Dayton, Orville is in Washington, and I am here in France. When something happens to one of the family, it is a terrible thing for us to be scattered around the world.

"Is this another ploy, Monsieur Wright?"
"Is this another one of those excuses not to fly?"
"Does this mean that the trials will be postponed?"

Icarus felt the power in his lateral muscles. Each time he flexed his wings, his biceps bulged.
As soon as he caught an up-draught, he made his move. He soared as high as he could, then he went into a dive and flapped his wings. He caught another up-draught and soared again. Then he looked down for a moment and was filled with glee. Down below, far, far below him, was his father, skimming the waves, a tiny bird about the size of a seagull or maybe a hummingbird.

I will fly higher, Icarus thought. It is easy enough to do. Now that my father has shown me how to fly, it is all so easy. All I need to do is to catch a series of up-draughts. That is all that the eagle does and he is majestic. It is like climbing a set of stairs. Up and up; higher and higher. So this is the secret that the birds have kept from humans for so many years!

"Does this mean, Monsieur Wright, that there will be no further flights?"

Orville and another in an accident! "Where did you hear this?" "It came to the newspaper office! We left and hurried out here! We thought that you could add something to our story of the news!" "The presses are printing the story now! The news will soon be in the newspapers on the street!" "Can you get me these newspapers? How soon will they be out? I must find out about my brother! Please, will someone in the crowd please find me a newspaper!"

Chapter 12
Orville Wright 4

Fort Myer, Virginia
September 17, 1908

An exciting day at Fort Myer.
Carrying a passenger. Lieutenant Thomas Selfridge. Everybody is thrilled to see that the flying machine can take two. It is one thing to thrill at what someone else can do. It is an even bigger thrill to realize that you too can fly through the air. There are hundreds here today. For most of them, only days ago there was no such thing as human flight.

Phaeton soared far above the earth. The horses of the Sun Chariot purred and pranced. The reins felt easy in his hands. The tracks were visible in the clouds and the wheels churned in the grooves of the middle way.
The world looked beautiful from here. For the first time in his life, he could see the whole known world at the very same time. The clouds looked wispy, and once in a while, when the clouds drifted a little apart, he could see roads and houses and ponds and fields and trees.

"Have you become used to seeing your name in all of the newspapers, Mr. Wright?"
"Are you amazed at the size of the crowds that throng the parade square?"
"It must be wonderful to realize that your demonstrations have been so well received?"

Relaxing in the reading room of the Cosmo Club in Washington. Relaxing as much as one can while constantly being plied with congratulations.
Attempting to catch up on the latest aviation news.
"No one seems to realize at this close range what a revolution the flights of Mr. Wright portend. The problem of human flight is solved, and it only remains to work out the details."
Finally we are getting our due as the inventors of the flying machine. We always

believed that things would come right if we only kept on.

It is surprising what a little success can do to attract a crowd. Third circuit of the field. About five o'clock in the evening. It seems that there are more people arriving all the time. I'm a little rusty at the controls. High winds and an engine overhaul means I haven't been aloft in five days.

"Do you realize, Mr. Wright, that everyone who is important in Washington is competing to be the first in their set to have seen one of your amazing flights?"

"Do you realize that the President's son was a witness to your inaugural demonstration?"

"Do you realize that the President himself is eager to meet you?"

This is wonderful, Phaeton thought. My father is getting old. He is very, very cautious, as only the old can be. He was worrying himself quite needlessly. It is typical of the gods. They assume that no human can possibly do what they can do. Then they tell humans that they are inferior, and that they must stay within their sphere. It is a conspiracy of low expectations. The gods look down on humans; the humans look up to the gods. And humans never learn what they can do.

I worry about Wilbur being alone.
His strength is in the singular pursuit of an ideal.
He will be besieged by well-wishers and curious aviators, prying newsmen and jealous rivals. He will be inundated with business offers that must be read with a careful eye for the faulty clause.
I do not believe that his personality will welcome success.

Making sure to keep well inside the buildings and the trees. A very short turning space, but I am managing. Three rounds of the practice field complete. Lieutenant Selfridge seems to be having quite a ride.

Relaxing in the reading room of the Cosmo Club in Washington. Relaxing as much as one can while constantly being introduced to important people.
Attempting to catch up on the latest aviation news.
"There is no doubt that the problem of aerial navigation has been solved. Mr. Wright will take his place in history as the man who has showed the world that mechanical flight is an assured success."
Finally we are getting our due as the inventors of the flying machine. We always believed that things would come right if we only kept on.

The senator lights a fine cigar. The smoking room of the Cosmo Club is crowded.
"I can see a Congressional Medal of Honour in your future, Mr. Wright. What you have done has brought untold honour to your native land."

"Are you competing with your brother, Mr. Wright?"
"Are the size of your crowds as big as the reports of his?"
"Will you try to prove that you are a better flier than he?"

Fourth round of the practice field. Everything is working as smoothly as can be. Every part of the Wright Flyer is humming in tune. Easing out a little bit. Making a wider turn this time. Swinging out over the top of the building where we store the machine. Must be about a height of a hundred or maybe one hundred and ten feet.

Phaeton looked down from his father's chariot and smiled.

On one side of the mountains it was raining, and on the other side there was a whole valley full of the glorious rays of the sun.

Why should we accept the logic of the gods? Humans are equal to the gods in every way. Someday perhaps, Apollo will be too old to do his work. He will need someone to take over and drive the Chariot of the Sun. Today, he will be able to see what I can do. Perhaps he will think of me when he gets too old to drive his route. I hope he will mention me to Zeus. They could have a ceremony and hand the reins to me. My father could give a speech about how pleased he was that the Chariot of the Sun was in good hands. I would be the first human to do the work of a god.

The cigar smoke curls towards the ceiling.

"My brother and I have been as one. There has never been a moment when we didn't eat and sleep and breathe the atmosphere of invention as if our minds were fused together. We not only share the same blood by birth, we share the same blood by the nature of our common pursuit."

The senator squints his eyes behind his cigar.

"I will not accept an award for myself alone."

Moving directly towards Arlington Cemetery. Lieutenant Lahm and Charles Taylor and others are waving gently as we pass over them. Lieutenant Selfridge grins and waves his arm in an arc to take in the splendid view in front of us and below us. Not many people have seen what we can see. Now what on earth is that? A bit of a pinging noise in the back of the machine.

Then suddenly, there was a jerk, and the reins grew tighter. The leather squeezed against Phaeton's hands and he felt some pain. His hands grew red, and he tried to lean forward and lighten the pressure. He tried to free his hands from the knot that was formed by the reins.

Then a bump, and he realized that something had happened. He looked back and his fears were realized. Somehow the horses had bumped the chariot out of the tracks that were laid in the clouds. This wasn't what he wanted. He had planned to stay in the wheel-ruts. He had planned to follow the path that his father had made.

The reading piles up at the Cosmo Club. We are being mentioned in every newspaper throughout the land.

An interview, in the Chicago Daily News, with Octave Chanute.

"I say that the concept of wing-warping has been worked on by many, many inventors since at least the time of the great Leonardo da Vinci. The brothers wrote to me that they had read my book. They wanted to use my idea of a biplane configuration. I was generous in my response. I turned over all of my data. Years of theories and calculations and pivotal experiments. I helped them all I could. It was they who appealed to me to share my ideas."

I miss the family back at home.

Home is our brother-Lorin, the family bookkeeper, keeping the columns straight and true on our expenses in pursuit of human flight.

Octave Chanute couldn't believe it when we told him that – despite the enormous expenses of Professor Langley; despite the offer to solicit financial help from Andrew Carnegie; despite the offers of financial assistance from Octave Chanute – we had no need to accept a single dime.

A glance behind me. Lieutenant Selfridge turns and looks back too. Nothing seems to be wrong. Everything is working smoothly. Yet still a clipping sound. A constant tap, as if something is hitting lightly against something else. Lieutenant Selfridge looks at me and points to his ear, indicating that he can hear it too. There must be something wrong.

Travelling back and forth between Washington and Fort Myer. Constantly being recognized as the man who is being featured in the newspaper headlines.

Attempting to catch up on the latest aviation news.

"If there is a Greek god to whom Mr. Wright can be compared we do not know of one. The stories of the gods are merely ones of imagination; the story of Mr. Wright, and his soaring machine is one of achievement."

Finally we are getting our due as the inventors of the flying machine. We always believed that things would come right if we only kept on.

Better to shut off the machine. Whatever the tapping sound there is something that shouldn't be hitting something else. I'll turn off the motor and drift down to a landing as soon as we turn around and face in a direction from which a landing can be made. Lieutenant Selfridge looks over his shoulder again and turns back and looks at me.

The horses climbed higher and higher with every snort. Phaeton couldn't believe his eyes. For the first time in his life, he could see what looked like it must be the end of the world. It wasn't like a table-top, as he had learned in school. It was like a big ball that probably had another side. He wondered what people would look like who lived around the corner of the world. Probably like us, he thought to himself. There can't be people who are not like us or they wouldn't be people.

There was a pain in his right knee which he had braced against the dash-board. The wind was so strong it threatened to tear the rays of the sun from his head.

Wilbur's success has been tremendous with his flying demonstrations in France.

He has had all of the success that we hoped that he would have. The crowds are thronging to watch him perform his feats, the newspaper headlines give great credit to Le Système Wright, and heads of state line up to shake his hand.

If only the business of selling the Flyer was safely concluded.

"Surely you and your brother don't always agree, Mr. Wright?"

"Surely you don't always think the same?"

"In the invention of the flying machine, Mr. Wright, I wonder who has had the best ideas?"

Circling around. Getting ready to shut off the levers so we can drift down. Two big thumps! A violent shaking of the machine! Something has to be broken but I can't tell what! Suddenly she veers to the right. I reach for the lever and shut off the motor. I try to steer but I get no response. One wing up and one wing down. I try to bring her back to level but the balancing lever doesn't seem to respond. A feeling of drifting helplessly through the air.

Phaeton was extremely worried. The horses were snorting and spitting out foam. The air began to grow cold and it was getting very difficult to breathe. He pulled back as hard as he could on the reins but to no avail. His hands were jerked ahead a few times, banging his knuckles on the gold leaf-work on the edge of the chariot. His feet grew bloody as he pressed them against the floor.

What was he to do? The horses seemed to be angry. The horses seemed to be mad. They were grinding at their bits. He could feel their anger as it made its way back through the reins.

I push and pull the levers but receive no response. Suddenly the machine takes a lurch towards the left as the right wing makes a sudden rise in the air. I move the lever to try to make her return herself to the level.

"You say your father and sister are in Dayton and your brother is in France?"
"Why has your family not accompanied you, Mr. Wright?"
"You are astounding the world and yet are here alone?"

The letters pile up at the Cosmo Club. I sort through the formidable pile and open one that is addressed in a familiar hand.

A letter from Octave Chanute. A reply to a letter of protest that we have sent to him.

"Yes, of course, I agree that your use of lines and cables to warp the wings was highly original. I agree that you deserve much credit for inventing that. But I must say that the idea of adjusting the wings was not yours to patent. The idea of adjusting the wings is as old as the birds. The idea of adjusting the wings is as ancient as Man. The secret of the birds and the adjustment of their wings can be found as far back as the drawings of Leonardo. You had no right to patent what belongs to all of mankind."

Suddenly, the machine jerks herself loose from the glide and starts to plunge in a hurry towards the ground. We are about fifty feet up and we are travelling almost perpendicularly down. Lieutenant Selfridge turns towards me and says "Oh! Oh!" in a voice I can barely hear.

I miss the family back at home.

Home is listening to Katharine's stories about Leonardo and the Ancient Greeks, and always – always – asking her to please include more details about the mechanics of their dreams of human flight.

Canvas? Leather? Feathers? Glue?

Man has felt close to flight for thousands of years but no one yet has flown. How exactly did the ancient aviators raise themselves off the ground?

I pull the rudder lever as far as I can but receive no response from the machine. I let the lever go and pull it back again. Nothing seems to work. The rudder is as far down as it can possibly go. The machine is plunging towards the ground. The pressure is bulging the cloth in billows between the ribs. The front elevator has always saved us. We should be drifting down slowly. We shouldn't be plunging downward but we are. Lieutenant Selfridge clutches the strut to keep from falling.

Travelling back and forth between Washington and Fort Myer. Constantly being hailed by friendly crowds. Attempting to catch up on the latest aviation news.
Glenn Curtiss is being quoted in The Washington Post.
"The flights of Mr. Wright are very interesting."
There are some who refuse to acknowledge our success. Praise is withheld for ulterior motives. There are those who refuse to give credit for what we have done. Some are preparing themselves for the patent-battles ahead.

I miss the family back at home.
Home is father warning us that even the church has those whose motives are not entirely pure. He asks Wilbur if he'd mind taking time out from our discussion – of dihedral wings, anhedral wings and aspect ratio design – to go over the books, once again, of the Church of the United Brethren in Christ.
If a snake can hide in a woodpile, then a Judas can certainly hide in the Church of Christ.

I worry about Wilbur being alone.
I do not believe that Wilbur has the personality to perform the delicate balancing act between the preparations of the demonstrations and the making of the business decisions.
Neither Wilbur nor I should ever work alone. We never should have agreed to separate.

Foam formed at the mouths of the horses as they clenched the bits between their teeth and tugged at the reins.
Phaeton had broken the promise to his father. He had gone outside the path. He was striking out into territory that was unknown.
He had also broken the promise that he made to his mother. She had made him swear an oath on her favourite blue rose. It was in a vase on the table as they ate their supper. He had promised her that his request to Apollo would be to ask for health and happiness and the comfort of a large family in his old age.

Fifty feet! Forty-five feet! Forty feet! Thirty-five feet! The font rudder is hardly changing our angle at all. We continue to fall almost perpendicularly. Thirty feet! Twenty-five feet! Suddenly, there is an amazing change. The machine begins to level! She begins to save herself! She begins to pull her nose up fairly fast!

Phaeton's hands were swelling up. His hands were growing white. There was no circulation at all. The wind was tearing at the rays of the sun that clung to his head. The air was getting colder. He could hardly breathe at all. The Chariot of the Sun was out of control.

Phaeton started to cry and he wished three things: that he had never known who his father was; that he had never asked his request; and that he had never seen the Horses of the Sun.

Please, Father, he prayed. I am sorry I asked for flight! Please get me down from up here in the sky!

"Don't you find all of this a little bit overwhelming, Mr. Wright?"

A few more feet and we'll be all right. A few more feet between us and the ground and we'll be able to flatten out and drift to a landing. But the ground is coming up rapidly! The ground is getting close! The skids dig in and we are plunging into the ground!

Chapter 13
The Wright Brothers 5

Kitty Hawk, North Carolina
December 17, 1903

A cold day at Kitty Hawk.
Ten thirty-five. The day is moving along. Boy, that wind sure tears at the struts and hums in the wires. "Hold on tight, everybody!" If those boys let go, she could tumble right off the track. Not sure they realize how delicate the whole situation is. This machine is bigger and heavier than any we've ever tested. The wind could tear her right off the rails. This wind is stronger than any we've ever had to face.

Prometheus stopped running for a moment and ducked in behind an over-hanging piece of rock. Mid-afternoon – hot sun and blinding light. Panting in his hurry; nervousness in his fear. He smeared his forearm across his face and the sweat was like honey. A tiny sound. What was that? He rolled his eyes around the rock and looked back to the top of the mountain, but nothing was there.
He held the torch out away from his body so as not to get burned. There was much more heat than he would have imagined. It would be hours yet until darkness. Plenty of time for him to descend if he were unnoticed. It was early yet, so the gods would continue to snore. A few more hours undetected and nothing on earth would ever be the same.
He moved out in the open, glanced over his shoulder and began to plunge downward again. He nicked his legs a couple of times on the sliding shale.

Another stunning surprise. Why has nobody been here before? We assumed all through the process – all through the solving of the mysteries of curvature and control, of lift and drag and drift, and power-to-weight ratios – that someone had developed a theory of propellers long ago.

The water we swim in; the air we breathe. Calculations in a notebook. Theory, speculation, tests and trials. To understand and control what has never been imagined before. To capture the forces of nature in an equation. To control the forces of nature by making objects in our workshop with our hands.

Gliding angle - fixed angles of attack - efficiency - contact with the air - varying speeds - changing angles of attack - stability - constancy - glide ratio - thrust.

Kitty Hawk is cold in mid-December. The rains fall hard and pock the ground and our footsteps freeze in puddles on the sand. The winds sweep in off the Atlantic and tug at the edges of the buildings. More than once, we have stood outside, coattails swirling around us, nails between our teeth, wielding a hammer in an attempt to strengthen the struts that keep our sheds from blowing away.

Kitty Hawk in mid-December makes us think of mid-December back at home.

What length? What width? What shape for these propellers? What dimensions for maximum transfer of power? No human being has ever figured this out.

How easy it would be, we assumed, to tap into what has been done. In marine technology, we thought, surely propellers have been developed which we can borrow to fly through the air.

After all, propellers have been powering boats for many years.

Angles of strike - efficiency of the angle of attack - blade area - length of blade - speed of rotation - maximum rpm - sprocket ratio of the gears - five-sixth from the hub - 23 to 8 - 8.5 feet.

We believe she is ready to fly. We have everything figured out. We have the numbers for everything that we could possibly need to know. The wings, the frame, the motor, the propellers, the horsepower, the lift, the wind. We have every number in harmony with every other number. Professor Langley might just be lucky, but we might just be right. As much as is humanly possible, we have squeezed the guesswork out of the invention of the flying machine.

Leonardo descended from the top of the hill. The pathway was worn, but there were places where one would stumble, if one wasn't alert. At times, it made good sense for an old fellow to sit down on a rock, ease his bag down, rub his aching hip and pause for a while to catch his breath.

Ah, the view of Florence. A view that never ceases to take the breath away. The bag with the notebook is certainly heavy. I am growing a little old, I think, to carry such a burden. Perhaps I should plan a little more. Not everything needs to be brought along every day. Perhaps tomorrow I shall carry a little less.

But then, perhaps I won't. My notebook is my notebook. It is the instrument with which I think. I wouldn't want to find myself unprepared.

What have they been doing all these years? What have the boat-builders been doing? They have just been putting each boat in the water, with any old propeller, and letting the power of the steam-engine push it forward as best it can. They have developed no theory of the shape and size that a propeller should be.

Two propellers - amount of torque - poundage of thrust - loss of blade performance - theoretical tangential angle of pressure - normal line of pressure - foot-per-second speed - miles per hour - minimum flying speed - approximate blade performance.

Home is where we will spend Christmas Day.

When we came here, to Kitty Hawk, in September, we never expected that we would still be here in mid-December.

We are very close to the first powered and controlled human flight. Nevertheless, we have decided that we will be home, no matter what, for Christmas Day.

Well, we can't afford to guess about propellers. We are not boat-builders, after all. We are very close to inventing the first human-carrying, powered machine that will ever fly. A boat will move inefficiently through the water, and not come to any harm, but an air machine without an efficient propeller will not allow for error.

We have the weight of the man and machine. We have the power of the motor. And if these are not in balance, the man and the machine will surely fail. If our propeller is inefficient, our flying machine will never leave the ground.

Throwdown - compressibility - effect of flowing air - throwdown loss - quadratic equations - acceleration - mass - weight - gravity - .075 foot pounds per cubic foot.

Evenings in the shed. Reading about Professor Langley by the light of the lamp. Another shake and a dribble of sand makes a pool on the knee. Why do the newspaper act as such a magnet for sand?

Professor Langley's second attempt to put a man-controlled flying machine into the air. He has vowed to do so by the end of the present year. A houseboat has been anchored in the Potomac River for use as a launching place. Fifty thousand Army dollars. Another twenty-five thousand dollars from the Smithsonian. The greatest minds and theories in science. A fifty-two horsepower engine. Forty-two-foot wings. An eight hundred and fifty pound machine. A better launch-rail than before. It was the launch-rail that snagged on the first attempt.

The professor gives his assurances: "Surely this will be the machine to begin a new age."

Everybody positioned. Removing the c-clamp from the bench that was balancing the wing. Holding her steady against the wind. When the hands let go, be ready for a sudden tug. The snarling sound of the motor. Impossible to hear. Hand-signals only from now on.

We realize now that water is not like air. The way in which a propeller will move through the air is not the way in which a propeller moves through the water. A marine propeller displaces a volume of water by pulling the water through and pushing it out at the back, but a propeller that moves through air does not pull anything. We have to start our study of the science of the air-propeller from the beginning and work everything out from there.

Once more, we are entirely on our own.

426 feet per second per second - one pound per square foot of disc area - one cubic foot of air - gross speed - sum of throwdown - forward velocity - value of throwdown - the positive root - propeller disc area - divided by two.

Home is the bicycle shop in Dayton, Ohio. 1127 West Third Street. A few blocks away from our other home on Hawthorne Street. The Wright Cycle Company. The brick building in front and the frame building in the back. The sale, rental and repair of bicycles. The invention of a machine for powered, controlled, human flight.

All within a dinner-time bicycle-ride from home.

Shaking the sand out of the newspaper and smoothing out the wrinkles. Studying the details in the newspaper one more time.

Professor Langley's flying machine leaves its launching place. The newspapers report the experiment to the world.

"On the signal to start, the airplane glided smoothly along the launching tramway until the end of the slide was reached. Then, left to itself, the airplane broke in two and turned completely over. The operator found himself under the water with the machine on top of him and with his cork-lined canvas jacket so caught up in the fitting of the framework that he could not dive downwards, while the floor of the aviator's car, which was pressing against his head, prevented him from coming upward."

Octave Chanute puffed at his pipe, trying doggedly to revive a dying flame.

"I have promoted your work in every way I could," he said. "I was the first to explain your advances to the French. I spoke to the Aero-Club de France. I wrote articles about you for L'Aérophile and Le Review des Sciences. I also had copies of your address to the Western Society of Civil Engineers printed and sent them off to everyone in Europe who was interested. I explained the wing-warping and the use of the vertical tail. I even offered to purchase the Ader machine from the French for you to work on, here, for me. I have made you celebrated all over Europe. Everyone in France who is attempting human flight is using what they call 'Le System Wright' for their gliders. You couldn't ask for a greater indication of your success."

Designing the first propeller to ever move a human through the air. What size? What shape? What materials?

Thinking, discussing, arguing. What if this? What if that? How to translate the power of the motor into thrust through the air? How to make eight horsepower into ninety pounds of thrust?

Volume - weight - density - 32 feet per second squared - 10 cubic feet of air - efficiency - total loss - torque - dynamic efficiency - formula.

The path was smooth and Leonardo followed it as it meandered downward in the afternoon sun. The city of Florence lay glowing as he made his way along the path.

To catch the late-afternoon sun in a glass of wine at a table in the Piazza della Signoria. To do this at the end of a tiring day, when the body has a hip that must be rubbed, when the mind has been perplexed, stretched as far as it can go, when something has lit a spark, kindled a flame, blew on a cinder, and stimulated the imaginative ink to flow. That kind of feeling is bellisimo. The very essence of what it is to be a man.

His throat was very dry. It was a wonderful transmutation when you thought about it. Alchemical in its working. How the grapes would capture the gold of the southern slopes.

Drawing must follow drawing. Idea must follow idea. There must be a way to capture on paper what I have imagined.

I believe I will have a glass of Antonio's best.

Ready to go. The motor barking and snarling. Getting angry at the wind, like a dog will do. The rattling of the chains. Not very far away from the ears. The buzzing whir of the propellers. Drowning out the sound of the wind. If it wasn't for the pressure on the face, we'd forget it was blowing.

So many things will be happening all at once.

The machine will be moving forward; the air will be moving backward; the propeller will be moving sideways.

At first look, it seems, there is nothing in this phenomenon which can be measured.

Loss from the slip - angles of attack - vacuum - end view - blade sections - testing machine - 29 explosions of the motor - lift in pounds - denominator - graphing.

Saturday is our busiest day in the bicycle shop.

"Walk in; ride out. You'll never regret the purchase of a Wright machine."

We sell the Coventry, Premier, Lyndhurst, Cleveland, Envoy, Fleetwing, Warwick, the Halladay-Temple and our very own bicycles, the Van Cleve and the Wright Special. Large tubing, high frame, tool steel bearings, needle wire spokes, narrow tread with brazed tubing for extra strength. A choice of metal or wooden wheels. Five coats of rubber-baked enamel, brush-coated in black or carmine, whichever your choice.

On less-busy days, we work on our flying machine.

Prometheus's sandals slid in the slippery shale.

Best to arrive at the bottom in daylight.

The torch blazed steadily with its flame. He held it out at arm's length and admired the latent power. If one of the gods should awake and yawn and shrug and scratch himself, and saunter over near the edge of the mountain, it wouldn't matter. The fire from the torch would probably not be noticed in the brightness of day.

The fire still blazed on the Olympic hearth -- that was the amazing thing. It was like air, in that regard, but not like water or rock. If some was removed it was immediately replaced again, so none of this strange new element would ever be missed. Perhaps he could keep his new secret forever. Perhaps the gods would never know. And how were gods the less if their fire still burned the same?

The shale gave way to sharp rock and jagged edges.

What happens to air when it is compressed?

What if a propeller moves too fast as it moves through the air? Will the machine reach the speed of the air and lose its power? At that point, will it stall and drop from the sky?

No one has ever known that these questions need answers. No one else has ever considered that these questions might even be asked.

Horsepower - thrust - pressure - bent end - power plant - velocity of rotation - tangent - maximum diameter - air pressure coefficient - static test.

"Ready!" Hard to hear in all the noise, but the hand-signal makes it clear. Pull the machine back a bit to ease the pressure against the rope. The lever to the left, the slipping of the rope and she's released. One of us holds onto the wing to keep her level. The wind must be about twenty-seven miles per hour.

The solution to the problem is to realize that the propeller is a rotary wing – a wing that moves in a spiral course, but still a wing.

A propeller on a flying machine does not pull air. It is the propeller that is being pulled. There is more pressure behind the propeller than there is in front. The vacuum in front will serve to pull the propeller along. This means that we can use the tables that we have developed for the wings.

Miles per hour - blade width - tables - sizes - canvas-covered tips - elevation - cambered surfaces - slow speed - line of resultant pressure - velocity in miles per hour.

The Wright bicycle shop.

A turret lathe, a drill press, a tube-cutting brake, an internal combustion engine to provide the power to the press and lathe. An electrical welding apparatus.

And for a few weeks, a wind tunnel, which allows us to uncover the thousand-year-old mystery of the shape of the human wing. Cutting two hundred different sizes and shapes of wing out of sheet-metal with the shears. Compressing the trials and errors of two hundred summers of guesswork into a six feet long by sixteen inch square box.

Only a few weeks, though, for the wind tunnel to take up space, as we have to go out the back door and around to the front of the shop in order to get inside the store to serve a customer.

Prometheus kept glancing back over his shoulder. His sandals swished through the grass. Sweat formed on his chest and dripped down from his chin.

A shepherd! Prometheus stopped, and crouched down in the grass. He didn't know whether he knew him. Too far away to be able to tell. He had taken a route that avoided the path where the gods might look for him.

What to do?

A sliver of twig fell off and singed his arm. He shook it off and held the torch away from his face. To carry a torch on a blazing-hot day was to double one's load.

Best to avoid the shepherd. He grazes his flocks this far up the mountain; he must come here every season; he would probably feel beholden to the gods. A different route would be judicious. He'll hear about what's happened soon enough; he'll be grateful when he knows; this is something that will affect every person in the world.

He swung the torch around, and crouching low to avoid detection, he moved off in another direction. In this situation, it would be better not to rely on the trust of another man.

What was it that was bothering Octave Chanute?

He got up in the morning and went out for a walk in the cold and then came back and said he couldn't stay for another day.

The most efficient curvature?
Estimated area? Rotational velocity? Angle of attack? Torque? Thrust? Blade-width? Planform? Slip? What are the answers to these questions?
When one thing changes, it changes all of the rest.

Percent of slip - average efficiency - shape - side view - taper tip - angle of incidence - blade element - 65 explosions of the motor - normal pressure - gliding angle.

Increasing in speed along the track. Seven or eight miles an hour. No misfire so far, but the resistance of the wind is holding her back. Can't be moving more than ten miles an hour. Ninety pounds of thrust should be enough at twenty-four miles per hour to allow her to leave the track. We're going to find out soon. The feet are kicking up the sand. Wind speed, ground speed, lift. Hope she's not too heavy to lift herself. The total weight crept up on us. Six twenty-five was what we hoped for, but the machine rose up to over seven hundred pounds.

From theory to design.
Two propellers, to minimize the vibration and maximize the volume of air being acted upon. Eight-and-a-half feet in length. Three laminations of spruce. The tips covered in fabric to keep from splitting. Light duck canvas seems to work best. Then a coat of aluminum paint. Mounted behind to minimize turbulence over the wings.

Rotational velocity - slip - materials - backward sweep - apparatus - perpendicular - normal line - propeller notebooks - resultant velocity - looks like we go with air foil number nine.

With our hands, and with our tools, in this bicycle shop at 1127 West Third Street, in Dayton Ohio, in our spare time – between bicycle seasons, and reading to our brother-Lorin's children, and assisting our Father in his times of tribulation, and going to church, and visiting the bank and the library and the grocer's and the butcher shop – we have invented the world's first self-powered, human carrying, controlled, practical flying machine.

Leonardo crossed the Arno on the Ponte Vecchio.
Many cities have their attractions, but Florence is unique. I only leave her of necessity, and only then, when I have promised her that I shall return.
The piazza will be drowsy in the late afternoon. Chickens and loaves of bread and blocks of cheese. Sandals and robes and spices from far-away lands. Chatter, on the best of topics, in the many cafés. Late vendors will seek to draw my eye. Many people will call "buon pomeriggio" and beckon me to join them, but I have work to do.
An empty table at Antonio's is what I am most in need of now. Oh, I am sure that I will find one. It will be another fine moment in the journey of an excellent day.

The transfer of the power of the motor.
A way to get the power of the motor to work on the air. Engine, crankshaft, sprocket and chains. Propeller shaft for the chains. A transmission ratio of twenty-three to

eight. A maximum use efficiency of 66% of the horsepower that is delivered to the propellers.

A formula for the design of a flying propeller. A formula which includes every variable which affects a machine which is designed to fly through the air.

Hatchet, plane, draw-knife.

We can't afford to make a propeller that is based on hopeful guesses. We have balanced out all of the numbers. We believe that this propeller – the one that we are carving and planing and shaping – will be the propeller that will move us through the air.

Late at night, in the cold of the shed, reading in the glow of the kerosene lamp. Pouring over the newspaper reports of the experiment of Professor Langley.

"Exerting all the strength he could muster, the operator succeeded in ripping the jacket entirely in two, and thus freeing himself from the fastening which had accidentally held him, he dived under the machine and swam under the water for some distance until he thought he was out from under the machine. Upon rising to the surface, his head came in contact with a block of ice which necessitated another dive to get free."

Octave Chanute stood shivering while he waited in the cold. His greatcoat was snugged at the neck with a tightened scarf. Beside him, Bill Tate was lifting the suitcase onto the cart. There was ice in the little ponds that the rain had made.

The cold made Octave Chanute seem very fragile. He was buried deep inside the hood of an enormous parka.

"Let me know how your attempt turns out," he said. "I shall be anxious to hear the news. By the way, have you allowed for the loss of power as it moves through the chain? There is usually quite a loss. I would allow for a thirty-percent loss of power if I were you."

Bill Tate turned and waited for Octave Chanute.

"But, if you are not successful this time, don't be disheartened or depressed. Don't let your failure undermine you, if it should come to pass. I have been thinking, lately, of some of my own designs for flying machines. You could always go back and work on some of those."

Our house at 7 Hawthorne Street, our bicycle shop at 1127 West Third Street, and our shed on the sands of the beach at Kitty Hawk.

These places are our home. Without a home, we could never leave the ground.

"Then one day," says Katharine, twisting around in her chair in the parlour, as we all look up abruptly from our various books. "Pegasus's rider angers the gods. No one knows what it is that the boy has said or done, but the gods send a gadfly to sting the winged horse. The rider is thrown to the earth, where he strikes his head on a rock. No one knows how badly he is injured, but many believe that the boy remounts and rides again."

Left hand on the lever. Wind burning against the face. Hope those nuts on the propeller-shafts stay tight. Moving the elevator control to nearly full-lift. Pulling the head back almost unconsciously. Hoping that little gesture will help to make her rise. Running alongside and holding the wing. The others all left behind. Couldn't trust anyone but ourselves to touch the machine. By the last quarter of the third rail the speed should be so great that she will outdistance the runner. Any moment now, the Flyer should lift herself up and into the air.

Chapter 14
Wilbur Wright 5

Le Mans, France
December 31, 1908

A sad day in France.
Climbing in among the wires of the Wright flyer. Settling into the seat on the front edge of the lower wing. Placing my feet on the bar in front.

Icarus couldn't see his father anymore. He had flown higher and higher with each up-draught. He wanted to enjoy the sensation of height. He was over the sea, so there wasn't much scenery.

He glanced back over his shoulder and was pleased to see that the island of King Minos was still visible. He could see everything in miniature. No human had ever seen the human world from this distance before. He could see the palace that King Minos thought would give him control of the island, the labyrinth that King Minos thought was impossible to escape from, and the little sailing ships that King Minos thought could stop anyone from leaving.

How foolish King Minos had been. How small his creations looked now.

Lieutenant Selfridge has died. He cracked his skull on impact and died one hour after reaching the hospital. He is the world's first air-crash victim.

Orville is alive. A fractured left leg, four broken ribs, a fractured and dislocated hip, a back injury.

Well, at least Orville is not alone. Katharine is in Washington with him as he heals.

It is a terrible thing for the family of Lieutenant Selfridge.

We knew that there would be risks. We have lived through many accidents. We have suffered bruised cheekbones, broken fingers and cut lips, but we have not had a major accident until this time.

Our secret has been to check and check again. I believe that the accident would not have happened if Orville and I had not been forced to work alone.

There is a difference between the night and the day.

During the day, there are successful flights and cheering crowds and flattering newspaper headlines. During the night there are nightmares of malfunctions of the machine and crippling accidents and of business deals gone wrong, and always the hollow experience of working alone.

I know that for Orville it must surely have been the same.

Thousands of people from all over the continent of Europe are coming to Le Mans. Former Prime Minster Balfour, of England, Lord Northcliffe, the Duke of Northumberland and even the King of Spain. They all want to take part in the dawning of the age of human flight.

I put them all on the end of the rope that lifts the weight to the catapult.

Monsieur Barthou, a French cabinet minister, has told me that the government of France will soon confer the Legion of Honour on me, for my contribution to the cause of human flight.

"Be assured, Monsieur Wright, that this award is an honour that is heart-felt by the people of France. What you have done, Monsieur Wright, will change the nature of the way that we all will live."

"What was the cause of your brother's accident, Monsieur Wright?"
"Were you aware that flying is a dangerous thing to do?"
"Had you known Lieutenant Selfridge very long?"

"Please realize," I told Monsieur Barthou, "that any awards, citations or proclamations that do not include both my brother and myself will be declined. Our accomplishments have all been the products of our working together."

Cold here at Le Mans. Snow on the field. I am looking forward to moving further south. Bundled in cap and gloves and winter coat. The competition makes me fly in less than ideal weather. Henri Farman has flown for forty-four minutes. I have flown for an hour and thirty-one minutes and twenty-five and four-fifths seconds. The competition is too close for me to relax. Today, despite the cold, I am determined to stay in the air for two hours or more.

Icarus flexed the tip of his wing and caught an up-draught. He looked down on the ant-like world of Man below.

Creations of Man, Icarus thought to himself, you cannot know how tiny you look from up above. Your size is your importance. How could you think that Man has any importance down there on earth?

To acquire importance, you must soar up close to the sun.

I will not accept any individual awards.

All of our planning has been as one. The turning of every nut, and the tightening of every wire has been done by the two of us. The inventor of the flying machine, and the pilot of every flight – no matter who has been on the ground or in the air – has been the Wright Brothers.

I wish we all could be together.

I wish that Orville and Katharine and Father and I could just be back at home, at 7 Hawthorne Street, sitting on the verandah, with no injuries, or regrets. Just sitting on the porch as it was in the early days, when we chatted and laughed and speculated about human flight.

Arranging the string in front of my chest. It is this string that will cut the engine off, instantly, should difficulties arise. When the body presses ahead, all power will cease.

The hill-like pile of letters on the table in the workshop. One stands out, amid the others, by the return-address of a former friend. I pour my cup of coffee. I sip and settle back.

Some thoughts, expressed in a letter from Octave Chanute.

"You gave the impression, in a newspaper article which I came across quite recently, that I had somehow thrust myself upon you, when you were starting out in your pursuit of human flight. I must ask you to please refrain from giving this false impression in future interviews. I am disappointed that I have to remind you of what are the facts. If you will only cast your memory back to those early days, you will recall that it was you who wrote to me and asked for help. It was you who initially solicited my advice."

The agony of human relationships.

What to say about Octave Chanute? If we praise him in the newspapers, we are reinforcing his claims that we are the clever tinkerers who breathed life into his ideas. If we fail to praise him, we are implying that he has contributed nothing to our invention of human flight.

Better to say very little, except what we have always said: that we are very, very grateful for his friendship.

Checking the controls for the hundredth time. Moving the levers forward and back. Everything seems to be in working order. Checking my coat-buttons to see that they are snug, and pulling my cap down hard to prevent its sudden loss. The men pull the rope that raises the weight on the catapult. 1600 pounds of counter-weight. As soon as they are ready, I will make my ascent.

Unable to sleep at night. Lighting the lantern in the shed, and shuffling through the stacks of newspapers on the bench.

"The accident in America has proven that the Wright accomplishment is not as significant as we had thought it to be. The accident proves that our own inventors are much closer to the Wright achievements than we had thought."

This is difficult to bear. Those who have praised us are having their sober second-thoughts. First they gave their praise and now they are taking it away.

"What were the factors that were involved in the fatal crash, Monsieur Wright?"

"Can you assure us, Monsieur Wright, that you have corrected the situation that led to the accident?"

"In view of the fatal accident, is not the future of flight still quite a long way off?"

There are days when I feel too sick to take to the air. I push myself out of the shed and wave to the thronging crowds and watch the men carefully as they prepare the waiting machine.

I spend an hour inspecting the entire machine while the newsmen ask their questions and the murmuring crowd grows restless and the workmen grow surly at what they take to be the unnecessary-checking of their work.

I climb between the wires and signal to the catapult men and go flying into the air once again.

But I am sick when I think of Orville and Lieutenant Selfridge. In spite of all of the adulation and the acceptance of our machine, I would rather all of us be home on the verandah at 7 Hawthorne Street.

I will stay in the air as long as I can today. I will win the Coupe Michelin. It will take perhaps two hours and many miles. The weather is very cold. I can see dark clouds in the sky. Possibly there will even be sleet or rain. My fingers will be numb inside my gloves. My cheeks will freeze and the cold will find its way inside my coat, perhaps, but I am determined. I will overcome Orville's accident. I am determined to fly for the both of us today. I am determined to break as many flying records as I can.

If only we knew the cause of Orville's accident. If only we knew what took Lieutenant Selfridge's life. A nut, a screw, a soft-spot in one of the pieces of wood? What caused the propeller to tap against the wire?

The heat began to sizzle in the feathers of Icarus's wings. The wax began to melt and gradually, one by one, the feathers began to fall off and drift below Icarus down through the sky.

Icarus looked down and noticed the soft white items in the air. It took him a while to realize what was happening.

I am losing feathers at a great rate, he thought, but I am still moving upward in the air. My father is very cautious. He used far too many feathers when he built the wings. No man has ever flown before. My father was groping in the dark when he made his decisions. Every idea needs some refinement. The wings feel better with what amounts to a lighter load.

"Was it the machine, Monsieur Wright, or was it the operator that was the cause of the fatal crash?"

"Should your brother have been left behind, to fly on his own?"

"Are you a better flyer than your brother, Monsieur Wright?"

Bending down and releasing the catch that holds the anchoring wire. A signal for the men at the catapult. The Flyer darts forward and I am in motion. A speeding train along the rail. I keep the elevator down to prevent early lifting. Then, half-way along the rail, I pull the lever back and the elevator starts to lift her and I am airborne. The whole machine raises bodily off the track. The speed of take-off is always a surprise. I am in the air, every time, in no more than an instant.

Icarus left a trail of floating feathers. The closer he got to the sun the more the wax kept melting on his wings. One by one, the feathers loosened and blew away.

Perhaps we could have flown faster and higher with lighter wings, he thought. I welcome the loss of the extra weight. It is not by addition, but by subtraction that man gains wisdom. The wings do not cease to be wings just because they are lighter. There is a point at which the optimum is reached. It is really a very simple question: how many feathers will allow a man to fly?

A head-ache in the night. Nothing to do but to light the lantern and read the newspapers.

"Monsieur Wright has certainly impressed, but there is nothing in what he has done that we cannot emulate. It will not be long, we believe, before we have surpassed what Monsieur Wright has managed to do."

This is difficult to bear. Those who have praised us are having their sober second-thoughts. First they give their praise and now they take it away.

"Why can you not solve the problem of the cause of your brother's accident, Monsieur Wright?"
"Is it not dangerous for you to fly in a similar machine?"
"Were you too quick to proclaim the age of human flight?"

A very gradual ascent. I always keep the Flyer close to the ground and mount to the higher levels very gradually. For someone watching from far away, she must seem to be travelling along the ground and not flying at all. But then, gradually, it will be obvious that she is being lifted by the wind as she slowly travels up the slope of the hill of air.

Unable to sleep a wink. Past mid-night. The coal-oil lantern gives a glow. Sitting on the stool in the shed at Le Mans. The cold of December finding its way in through the cracks. Reading the latest comments in the newspapers.

"Delagrange, the Brothers Voisin, Farman, Santos-Dumont, Blériot – all are working diligently on flying machines which they believe are an improvement on Le Système Wright. With all of these illustrious inventors working on the question of human flight, it is only a matter to time before our own inventors and aviators will reign supreme."

This is difficult to bear. Those who have praised us are having their sober second-thoughts. First they give their praise and now they take it away.

"What did you do that Clement Ader had not done before you, Monsieur Wright?"
"Did you not simply apply your mechanical skills to Chanute's ideas?"
"Is it not true, Monsieur Wright, that you have no more ownership of these ideas than anyone else?"

How pleasant it would be to be bending over a bicycle, in the shop at 1127 West Third Street, in Dayton Ohio, mending a flat tire for a boy who only wants to get on his bicycle and flee the heat of town, to ride out to the Pinnacles where the birds circle lazily by the hour.

It would be tempting to take my own bicycle and join the boy on his ride. What a wonderful way to spend an afternoon.

I picture an elevated track. An imaginary path. That I can ascend on my way upwards into the air. I try to keep her steady though occasionally she is buffeted and I must struggle to keep her right. Occasionally, a wave of air will give me a smack, like a wave on the Kitty Hawk beach. As in the water, I must search to regain my footing.

Icarus caught an up-draught and soared even higher.

Someday, Father will be pleased with me if I just steady my mind and stay the course. I will be the first human to look in the face of the sun. I will report back on what I see for the benefit of all mankind. The gods have kept their secrets for far too long.

Awakening from a night-sweat. Lighting the lantern and reading the newspapers once again.

"The question as to who has invented the flying machine is a debatable point. There are many French inventors who could make that claim. However, it is not in the invention or even in the art of flying that we are determined to compete with the feats of the Wrights. Very shortly, we are sure, we will have flying machines which will outdo the Wrights in the arena of the marketplace."

This is difficult to bear. Those who have praised us are having their sober second-thoughts. First they give their praise and now they take it away.

"Are there not currents and backwaters and eddies, Monsieur Wright, that defy your attempts at control of the air?"

"Is the sky not just as mysterious now as it has been since the beginning of the world?"

"Have you not been a little complacent with your claims that man has finally learned to fly?"

Then I must move my hands very subtly, to right the disequilibrium and to bring the tilting flyer back to the level. If I am subtle in my moves, the Flyer will seem to be constantly adjusting herself, like a bicycle that seems to balance independently of the rider. I must constantly readjust control in such a way as to ensure smooth flying. My movements should be invisible from the ground.

The hours are long and the work is tiring. I force myself to take a break. I sip my coffee and read a letter from Octave Chanute.

"It is my feeling that I have not been given the proper consideration for such aid as I might have furnished in your enterprise. Am I to believe that the pioneering work that I have done – most of it long before you ever showed an interest in the flight of man – has not been fundamental in the achievement of your success? If I believe this then I believe that I have failed."

The coffee tastes very bitter. Sometimes the break is much more tiring than the work.

If you don't have family, you don't have anything. That is what father always says, and he is right.

Sitting on the verandah. Orv and I in high debate about the merits of the various cambers of the wings. Father reaching for the sugar bowl and Katharine telling tales of antique flight.

If you cannot picture yourself sitting with someone on the verandah in the twilight – amid the laughter and the chatter and the endless cups of tea – then the person cannot be someone whom you could call a friend.

There was a day when we sat on the verandah with Octave Chanute.

Reaching the end of the grounds. Going into a gentle turn. Banking the flying machine so the turn is gentle and smooth. Leaning gracefully into the turn like a huge Kitty Hawk gull, soaring in an endless arc out over the waves.

Icarus grew tired and his wings grew heavy but he persevered. He was worried about the feathers as he looked along each shoulder and watched the departures. Puffs of feathers fluttered in the breeze and slipped away.

The hot wax melted and ran down the feathers and dripped down unto the twigs that were the frames of the wings.

He perspired as the dream unravelled. There were tear-drops forming on his face. A tear from each eye found its way onto each cheek and the force of the wind blew them back towards his ears.

"Does your brother's accident not prove, Monsieur Wright, that there is more to human flight than you have considered?"

"Are there not mysteries of size and weight and shape that resist your experiments?"

"Is there not something in the air that does not want human beings to learn to fly?"

There is no doubt in my mind that the accident which I suffered to my arm and the accident that Orville suffered in the death of Lieutenant Selfridge were due to the fact that we are working on our own. When we are together, we are not perfect – there were many bruised cheekbones, sore ribs and black eyes during the invention of the Flyer – but there is no doubt that we are much better together than when we are apart.

Neither Orville nor I will ever again work alone. We will never again agree to separate.

What was the cause of Orville's accident? What was it that caused the whole enterprise to crash?

There must be something in a nut or a screw or in the anchoring of a support-wire that is ready, at any time, to undermine our control of the air. If only we were together. With hours and hours of discussion, we could go over the performance of every piece of wood and metal and fabric in the machine.

Together, we could solve the problem that is causing both of us to lose our sleep.

My family will soon be here.

I look forward to the day when I will see them. As soon as Orville is able to travel, he and Katharine will take a boat to France. It will be wonderful to be together again. To think and act as one. To fine-tune the machine each time we fly. To adjust our invention to make it the finest flying machine that we can imagine. To combat the barrage of questions, and sort through the myriad contract offers. To be able to be two people acting as one.

It will be nice to be at one with Orville and Katharine again. I only wish that Father could be here too.

Maintaining equilibrium. Always aiming at the fine point between climbing and dipping, between turning left and turning right, between pitching-up and pitching-down. Riding the air as on a bicycle, smoothing out the combative turbulence, skimming the ripples and backwaters and eddies that are the always-nudging currents of the air.

Icarus started to fall. He ceased to climb towards the sun and came to a stop. He lost power and started to slide backwards towards the earth. One wing dipped low and he tried to correct it, as he had done before, by a subtle flick of the tip at the end of one wing.

The movement failed and Icarus went into a spin. He hurtled downward at great speed toward the sea. The sun glinted on what was left of the little white feathers.

I'm sorry, Father, he thought. I am truly sorry.

Icarus tumbled over and over as he fell from the sky.

"Have you managed to do some sightseeing, Monsieur Wright?"

Sometimes above the treetops. Sometimes dipping down. Sometimes five or six feet only above the ground. The engine buzzing steadily and the propellers humming behind me. Soaring triumphantly over the grandstand. The people are waving in silence. I can see, but not hear, the enthusiasm of the crowd.

Chapter 15
Orville Wright 5

Atlantic Ocean
January 10, 1909

Somewhere on the Atlantic Ocean.

Icebergs all around. The iceberg season is obviously in full swing. So beautiful yet so dangerous. How is it that the captain is able to find his way? Is it possible to keep our distance and come to no harm?

The Chariot of the Sun careened madly out of control. Phaeton's hands were bleeding. The reins bit into his palms. He pulled back on the reins and shouted, but it did no good.

The horses plunged up high and then down low. The chariot singed the heavens and scorched a path along the earth. The clouds had smoke belching from them and mountain tops were blazing with flames of fire.

The plants withered in the fields. The leaves of the trees took fire and the harvest smouldered. The sea opened up and swallowed islands and the shores were battered by gigantic waves. Where it had been dry there were mountains of water and where it had been water the land was parched and cracked. Deserts appeared, with acres of blowing sand, and the people who pointed at them didn't have a word for desert that they could use.

I worry about Wilbur being alone.

I worry about the one little unnoticed item that is lying in wait, for an inattentive moment, or a hurried attempt to fly or a distraction that undermines the attention. I am sure that my accident would never have happened if Wilbur had been at Fort Myer.

I feel the pressure of the blood in my legs and feet. The lack of use has made them useless. What a wonderful thing it will be when I can walk unaided again. I wish I could say the same for Lieutenant Selfridge. He is the first human being to die in a flying-machine crash.

Phaeton's wrists were on fire and the reins were slippery with his blood. The sun-rays on his head had tilted over one eye but he couldn't free a hand to push them back.

The horses soared and plunged their way around the globe. When they saw groups of people they would dive and scatter them in droves and burn their houses. Whole cities were destroyed and groups of people were instantly turned to ashes. The air was like a furnace. People burned from the inside, from the fires in their lungs. People wet handkerchiefs and put them on their faces. They fled to the hills and got caught in crowds that swelled the roads. They looked up at the sky in fear. Destruction was raining down on them from the air.

High on Mount Olympus, the great Zeus stood by the fire-pit, and looked up at the sky. A guard was pointing up into the clouds. Zeus squinted and put his hand up over his eyes. Then he shouted back into the palace for the other gods.

"Did you attend the funeral of Lieutenant Selfridge, Mr. Wright?"
"Did you speak to his family at the internment?"
"Does it bother you to have to walk with canes?"

I miss the family back at home.
It is wonderful having Katharine on the ship.
Home is Katharine and her stories, as she prepares her lessons on the Ancient gods and heroes. Home is asking Katharine to come out on the verandah to see what we have devised. She is wary as we tie the blindfold on, but she laughs when she sees our latest aeronautical breakthrough: a pillow-full of feathers and a pot of glue.

I can never seem to sleep. I must have tossed and turned all night. This morning my pillow was soaking wet and my head was aching. I have been forced to endure that terrible nightmare again.

I am so glad that Katharine is on the ship with me. She is helping me with the massive correspondence. It is impossible for me to write. Every second letter is a telegram which I dictate to Wilbur. He must be wondering what to look for. He must be studying his machine and wondering what – among the many components under suspicion – is the hidden flaw that is undermining our design.

I want to tell him everything I can about what went wrong.

All of the latest newspapers in the ship's library. The newspapers are full of stories on the flying craze.

The Ligue Nationale Aérienne has been formed in France, to try to find a French inventor for the flying machine.

"If the truth be known, it was Clement Ader who first indicated the means by which humans could attain controlled flight, in his Avion of 1897. Surely Ader's plan of running one propeller faster than the other, when a turn of the machine is desired, is not only earlier than the Wright invention of wing warping but far superior."

Those who have praised us are now dismissing us. They will not rest until they have undermined our claims. No doubt the darkest days are still ahead.

The Ader Avion was far too light to hold its shape in buffeting winds, but Clement Ader never knew. The Ader design was one that only worked on paper. Witnesses say that the Ader Avion never left the ground.

The patent courts have a bitter sense of humour. We must not only prove that our designs are the basis of all human flight, we must be prepared to prove what the owners of the other designs never got far enough to discover: that their designs – had they ever left the ground – would have proven to be fundamentally and aerodynamically unsound.

If we are to win in the patent courts we must be prepared. We must know much more about the designs of our rivals than our rivals have ever known about their designs themselves.

What to write to Wilbur?

It has been impossible to figure out what went wrong. I can only come close to an explanation. I believe that a stay-wire was torn loose by the propeller. The rear rudder, without the stay-wire, fell over on its side and was held there by the pressure on the under-side. The deviation from the true was so great that the front elevator could not overcome it.

But what was it that made the propeller reach out and tap the stay-wire?

Cold in the open air. The icebergs drift lazily on by, with a warning of subtle menace. When do the time-zones change? Surely the time-zones change somewhere between New York and France. What time would it be now? I feel suspended between two times. Perhaps, with my watch, I could do the math. I can't believe I have forgotten to wear my pocket-watch.

"It isn't Apollo, Mighty Zeus!" someone shouted.

"Well who could it possibly be then?" Zeus demanded. "It couldn't be anyone else! Have all of you gone mad? There is only one who is ever allowed to drive the Chariot of the Sun!"

"It is my son," a voice called, and the crowd parted. Apollo made his way to the front and hung his head. He looked different now that his head was barren of rays. "I apologize, O Zeus. I made a foolish promise to a maid. I said that I would grant a wish to any child that she might have, if only she would grant a wish to me. It is that child who is driving the Chariot of the Sun."

I had pieces of the wreckage brought for me to examine while I was in my hospital bed. It is difficult to figure it out alone. If Wilbur had been with me, we would have put hours into the detective-work. We would have gone through every moment of the accident and every nut and bolt and screw and piece of wood that constitutes the makeup of the machine.

Together we would have figured out what went wrong.

"Were you competing with your brother, Mr. Wright?"
"Did you take chances in your eagerness to outdo him?"
"Are you not afraid that your brother will get ahead of you while you are incapacitated?"

Alone in my state-room on the boat.

There are certain things that I keep with me and read again.

A letter from Octave Chanute.

"Is there not – somewhere in the many gliders that I have designed and constructed; somewhere in the many tables of calculations that I have compiled; somewhere in the many ideas that I have recorded – the key that allowed the two of you to tinker your way to success? Am I to be given so little credit for such a substantial contribution to what should be regarded as a communal result?"

The pain of human relationships.

We followed all of the early inventors until we found them stuck at barriers that they could not conceive the nature of, let alone devise the means to overcome.

What to say about Octave Chanute?

To say that his wings were incapable of flight is to sound ungrateful; to say that his wings were capable of flight is to tell an untruth. We refuse to acknowledge his public claims that we have succeeded with his ideas and not our own. His wing design contributed strength to our wings for sure, but nothing to their ability to fly. He beckoned us backwards when he continued to insist that we work on his designs.

It's best to say as little as we can.

I cannot walk without the aid of two crutches. A masseur pummels me for an hour or two each day. I am determined to walk without crutches in a week or so. There are bound to be newspaper photographers who will meet us when we dock. I don't want to be seen to hobble when I land in France.

I must try to figure out what to telegraph to Wilbur. I must tell him what I understand about the reasons for the crash. I will ask Katharine to help me to explain what Wilbur should know.

A telegram is a limited number of words; a telegram is not a conversation; the silence of a telegram does not confide.

I yearn for the time when Wilbur and I can talk.

"You did what?" Zeus demanded. "Do you realize what you've done? We are not safe here on Olympus! If this continues, the frame of the world will collapse, and we will fall into the turmoil of the ancient Chaos! Is there any way that you can right this wrong?"

"The answer saddens me to say," said Apollo. "There is only one way, O Zeus. Destruction demands destruction; fire must be combatted with fire. You are the only one who can bring this destruction to an end."

Standing in the prow and watching the icebergs that dot our path. This has to be the lowest point in the whole adventure. An accident without a probable cause; patent protection which is dragging us to court; pretend-inventors who are soaring on our wings; business offers which will make our partners rich; the French insistence that our invention is not our own. If there was a lower point than this, I cannot remember it.

"Has the Army rejected your proposal, Mr. Wright?"

"Does the accident mean that you have failed to prove your case?"

"Does this not prove that your invention should be placed in a similar category to that of the failed dream of Professor Langley?"

Resting my legs in the reading room of the ship's library. People bring me newspapers that are filled with the flying craze.

The Ligue Nationale Aérienne will not rest until it comes up with a French qualifier as the inventor of the means of human flight.

"We believe that the idea of Louis Mouillinard of slowing one wing to cause a turn was the idea that preceded the Wright idea of wing-warping."

Those who have praised us are now dismissing us. They will not rest until they have undermined our claims. No doubt the darkest days are still ahead.

Louis Mouillinard would have found that his system would induce a reverse-turn. Unless one banks the flying machine and controls the resultant reverse-turn with a movable rudder, as we were forced to figure out how to do, the design will fail.

Louis Mouillinard never faced the problem of the reverse-turn, as we did so long ago, because the Mouillinard design was never flown.

Everyone who has ever scribbled on a napkin is now being claimed as the inventor of human flight.

Why is it, then, that none of our predecessors managed to build a flying machine that could actually fly?

If ink and paper were all that was needed, man would have been flying for at least a thousand years.

Those inventors who are flying now have been given Le Système Wright by Octave Chanute. They have pole-vaulted over the logic of the machine that they claim to have invented. None of them has been forced to figure out the science of a flying machine while engaged in active flight. We have encountered phenomena that these people have not even wondered at. They would not be flying without the solutions that we have provided. Things happen in the air that cannot be guessed.

I have barely closed my eyes since we left New York. And yet I must have dreamed for hours about a Greek god. No, wait, perhaps it wasn't a god. Perhaps it was a mortal. It must be the father who was a god. I will have to ask Katharine about that old story when breakfast-time comes.

"Bring me a thunderbolt, and do it quickly!" Zeus cried. A guard turned and ran towards the palace. "This has gone on long enough!" Zeus shouted after him. "To make sure, perhaps you'd better bring me two!"

The gods all grew silent. Apollo turned to the wall; he had moved in under the portico; he was standing just beside the palace door.

Zeus selected one of the thunderbolts. Then he swung it two or three times to loosen his arm. Then he reared back until the tip of the thunderbolt almost touched the ground and then, with a grunt, he reared forward and let the thunderbolt fly.

How many more days until we reach the dock? How many hours from the dock to Paris? How many more to Le Mans? I've forgotten where Wilbur wrote that he would meet us. Katharine will know. I will ask her as soon as I see her, but it will be hours yet until breakfast. Why does everything slip away when you are asleep?

Phaeton's face was black as a cinder. There was blood streaming out of his eyes. The wind tore at his cheeks and at his eyelids. His hands were a pulp of mashed meat in the knot of the reins and his feet were torn to shreds on the chariot floor.

The horses foamed at the mouth and crunched the bits between their teeth. They reared and plunged through the heavens and then they dove like screaming banshees towards the earth.

"Has it occurred to you, Mr. Wright, that people will never want to fly if there is danger?"

"Will you accident put an end to your program for good?"

"Do you feel, in light of your accident, that the pursuit of human flight has been pretty much of a mistake?"

There are many people on the ship who wish to talk. There are many people on the ship who wish to offer condolences about the accident, or congratulations on the invention of human flight, or to mention Wilbur's latest foray into the uncharted skies. It is difficult to avoid people on a ship. It is easiest to avoid them in the cold outside. It is easiest in the early hours of the morning.

Passengers tip their hats and say hello, as I move along the corridors. Have I read the latest news of the flying craze?

A statement from Glenn Curtiss.

"No doubt the Langley Aerodrome was capable of flight. If it had flown, in December 1903, it would have preceded the Wright claims by nine days. It was prevented from flying not by inferior aeronautics but by an uncooperative launching rail and the collapse of the Langley financing. No doubt the Langley Aerodrome was capable of flight."

Professor Langley had not studied the birds. His wings were shaped like those of a buzzard. Ours are shaped like those of a gull. He had not noticed that a gull can fly in the strongest winds while a buzzard cannot.

The Langley Aerodrome was unsound, but doubt is Glenn Curtiss's greatest ally. He will stop at nothing to undermine our rightful claims. No doubt the darkest days are still ahead.

I miss the family back at home.

Home is father and a warning. There is no one, he says – as he spoons his sugar into his tea or pauses to clean his glasses with a handkerchief – who will treat you like your own. There is no one who will keep the faith with you who isn't as close to you as your own flesh and blood.

A Wright is the only partner you can trust.

Remember that when you go out to sell your machine.

Alone in my state-room on the ship.

There are certain things that I keep with me and read again.

A letter from Octave Chanute.

"My health is bad. I plan to travel abroad, in search of a much-needed rest. I regret some of the things that I have said, though not, or course, others. Perhaps when I am well again, we can meet, personally, the three of us, and talk at length. No doubt the days when we all shared a sense of adventure together – the days when the wind and the cold of Kitty Hawk could not stifle the warmth of our mutual quest – cannot be recaptured. However, there is no doubt they were better days than what these days have become. Perhaps some talk of the past will help to heal the wounds of the present. If there is any chance at all, I hope that we can resume the footing of our former and friendlier relations."

"Is your brother not flying in the same design of machine that you were flying, Mr. Wright?"
"Is his life not in danger, and those of his passengers too?"
"Is he not mistaken to continue to fly in France?"

How is it possible to go without sleeping and still have nightmares? I have noticed this phenomenon before. The number of times I fumble for my missing watch, as the ship rears and plunges as it struggles with the waves, means that I have had almost no sleep at all.

Phaeton tried to warn all those below. His lips were bleeding and his tongue was swollen but he shouted as loudly as he could. Through blackened teeth, he screamed in the face of the tearing wind.
"I apologize to everyone below me! I am sorry for what I have done! I have never seen destruction on such a massive scale! Oh Father, please forgive me! I didn't know what it was to want to fly! Oh please end this terrible nightmare! Do whatever you have to do to get me down!"

I worry about Wilbur being alone.
The only two accidents of any consequence in ten long years of working together happened when we were apart. Neither Wilbur nor I should ever have worked alone. We will never work apart, ever again.

The passengers are very kind. They bring me stories that they assume I would like to read.
An announcement from Glenn Curtiss.
"I am planning to revive the Langley Aerodrome, of December 1903. I am convinced that it will fly. When it does, I am sure that it will put to rest the claims that the Wright Brothers were the first to invent the means of human flight. I have no doubt that the Langley Aerodrome will fly."
We do not trust Glenn Curtiss. We must check his version of the Langley Aerodrome to make sure that does not alter it to comply with the knowledge that has been gathered since that time – knowledge that will be based on our inventions. The wings of the Langley Aerodrome were not scientific. Glenn Curtiss will have to use our system to make it fly – to confuse the courts and undermine the spirit of our patent.
No doubt the darkest days are still ahead.

Empty deck. Chairs stacked on the promenade. The cold air aggravates my injuries. Wilbur has arranged to move his flights to the south of France. I will ask Katharine to remind me of the name of the town. Too cold to stay outside; too miserable to stay inside. Too many people asking how I feel.

The thunderbolt glinted as it tore its way through a cloud. Phaeton was struck in the back and the thunderbolt went through him. He twitched like a pinned reptile and his chest exploded in a shower of his blood.
The rays fell off his head. The hands were loosened in the reins. Phaeton tumbled from the chariot. His hair was on fire as he cart-wheeled through the air.

I miss the family back at home.
Home is the cradle of all good news.
Home is Lorin, our brother and family bookkeeper, sitting down with Wilbur and meand going over the books.
We have paid for the whole adventure by ourselves.
From start to finish, Lorin tells us – from the first kite, in 1899, to the powered flight at Kitty Hawk in December 1903 – the quest for human flight has cost us less than a thousand dollars.

"And are you enjoying the pleasures of the voyage, Mr. Wright?"

Pacing up and down the cold deck with the aid of two canes. First the prow and then the stern. Watching the icebergs dotted ahead and then the turbulent wake behind. I can't wait to talk to Wilbur. It is going to happen soon. Very soon we will be landing safely in France.

Chapter 16
The Wright Brothers 6

Kitty Hawk, North Carolina
December 17, 1903

Pau, France
March 15, 1909

December 17, 1903. A cold day at Kitty Hawk.
Entering the fourth rail of track. About forty feet along. The front end turning up. Trying not to turn her up too sharply. Holding steady on the lever. The machine rising up to about ten feet above the track.

Prometheus strode down the sloping hill. The torch burned hot and he had to hold it out at arm's length. More than once now, he had singed the hair on his fore-arm.

He had decided that it would be best to stay out of sight until nightfall. The torch would not be noticed during the day.

I'll ask everyone to share the burden, Prometheus thought. Together we will defy the gods. If every human stands together, whatever the gods may do, they will have to do to everyone together. If every human stands together, we can begin a whole new era for our earth.

March 15, 1909. A pleasant day in France.
We have moved south – to Pau – to catch the warmth of the sun.
We are together again. And our sister-Katherine is with us. We have written to Father, back home in Dayton, and asked him to share the news with Lorin and the other members of the family. The Wright Brothers are back together, again, as one.

Leonardo limped across the Piazza della Signoria. It was early evening and he was tired. The straps of the bag that held his notebook bit into his shoulder, He paused a moment and shifted the strap from shoulder to shoulder one more time.

The sun was reluctant to leave the buildings of its favourite city. There is no greater beauty than the Florence of the setting sun.

A productive day, but there is so much more to do.

The tables were crowded in the Piazza della Signoria and there was a breeze, but each candle was protected by a cover of glass. People called to Leonardo and beckoned for him to join them as he limped his way along.

"Grazia, no, grazia. I have some work to do."

Surely Antonio would have a table where he could sit and work alone.

A cold day at Kitty Hawk.

The Wright Flyer rising off the ground. Leaving the track behind. Everyone shouting and halloing as she separates herself from the track. The shouting is a help. Hard to tell the exact moment when we become airborne.

Katharine's skirts are being tied. The hobble skirt – a dress-style derived of necessity – has become the fashion rage here in France.

There are two seats on the Wright Flyer. One for the pilot and one for the passenger. We promised Father, long ago, that the Wright Brothers would never fly together, but that promise made no mention of our sister-Katharine.

Years ago, we tossed a coin, and both of us won. We have rotated our roles ever since. Though one of us will accompany her, and one will remain on the ground, it is the Wright Brothers who are the pilot of every flight.

A pleasant day in France.

Together again. The two of us as one. We are flying before the world. We are demonstrating our superiority to the other inventors. We have given the world its first practical flying machine. We have been acknowledged by all and sundry. Captains of industry, heads of state. King Alfonso of Spain, King Edward of England, King Victor Emmanuel of Italy. We have landed at the feet of kings and they have stepped backward.

It was the size of the screws in the propeller-housing that caused the accident. We talked it over and figured out what it had to be. We have put hours into the detective work and now we feel that we know. We went through every moment of the accident and the performance of every nut and bolt and screw that constitutes the make-up of our machine.

We have concluded that it was the size of the screws that caused the accident. The vibration of the engine gradually worked the screws loose on the propeller-housing and the propeller tipped forward and tapped against the support-wire. That was the tapping noise that preceded the fatal crash.

The tapping broke the propeller, and this caused it to spin out of balance, which caused a strong vibration, which further loosened the housing of the propeller shaft, which then leaned forward and cut the support-wire.

The tapping noise was the propeller cutting through the wire.

The solution is very simple.

We need bigger screws in the propeller-housing. This will keep the vibration from working the propeller loose.

One adjustment and we can move forward in our attempt to finally achieve control of the air.

The propellers biting into the Kitty Hawk wind. The wings sucking us up higher into the air. We are right about where the camera was aimed. I hope John doesn't get too flustered to squeeze the bulb and snap the shutter. Be a shame if he should miss capturing what we have done.

Home for Christmas.
We have decided that whether we fly or whether we do not fly, we will leave Kitty Hawk in time to be home for Christmas. Whether we are the first to achieve powered and controlled human flight or not, we will be back in Dayton in time to celebrate Christmas with our family.
If necessary, history can wait for another year.

Katharine settles comfortably beside us in the flying machine at Pau. Her skirts are hobbled against the wind and she is smiling. The men pull steadily on the catapult rope. The 1600 pound weight moves up the derrick. All is ready. The crowd is paused and waiting. Then a signal and we are instantly in the air.

Mother would have been so pleased. She was always so mechanically inclined. It would have been wonderful for her to see what we have achieved. It was Mother who made our toys and built us a sled that year for Christmas.
Christmas with Mother was always a wonderful time of year.

Father is very proud of what we have accomplished.
The family joke is that Father should be tied to his desk and chair when things need mending around the house. Mother always said that if left to his own devices, Father would end up driving the hammer with the nail.
Father has contributed to us in other ways than mechanical. Books and numbers are Father's family contribution.

Very difficult to control. A strong Kitty Hawk wind and a touchy front elevator. Up to about ten feet high. Then dipping down to about five feet above the sand. Then responding to the adjustment of the elevator and coming up again.

Mother's hands and Father's books have led us to this moment in the air.

At Pau, the flying machine is being invented as we fly. We try to keep what works and change what we know can be improved. But a flying machine is a harmony of disparate elements. When one item is altered the behaviour of every other item is altered as well. One change can mean a completely different machine. With the new front-elevator design, we have gained and we have lost.

Christmas dinner at Lorin's.
Ever since Mother died, we have gone to Lorin's house for Christmas dinner, only blocks away from 7 Hawthorne Street.
Pop and Ullem and Bubs and Swesterchen. Lorin and Netta and Milton and

Ivonette and Leontine and Horace. With father saying grace and everyone saying, "Amen."

Father thanking the Lord for our good fortune, not forgetting the unfortunate who have no home on this day of celebration of our Lord's birth.

Ten of us around the table, with frost on the windows and snow out on the lawn, and the jingle of bells as the cutters glide up and down the street.

Mouths open, forks in hand, bibs on the children, while one of us – Uncle Will or Uncle Orv – carves the turkey.

No matter which one carves, it is the Wright Brothers who are carving the Christmas turkey

A steaming platter of turkey. And cranberry sauce in Mother's cut-glass dish. And the gravy, thick and brown, so thick that it seems reluctant to leave the gravy bowl; almost re-defining the human experience of gravity. Corn, bright and hot, and beans and peas and carrots brazed in the pan.

Presents and songs and hymns and a shadowgraph show, with Sam Bonebrake and Jim Higgenbotham, two sheet-metal characters whom we made for the children on a rainy day in the bicycle shop, and the tree – always the tree – with candles on the branches and an angel on the top.

Yes, we are determined that we will be home for Christmas Day.

A flying machine under its own power. Taking off from a standing start. From a track laid on a trough in the Kitty Hawk sand. Not relying on gravity to keep it aloft. Under the reasonable control of the pilot. This has to be powered flight. This has to be it!

Octave Chanute left Kitty Hawk a month before the flight. After forty years of yearning for man to rise above the earth and fly, he complained that Kitty Hawk in December would be far too cold for him to stay.

We are testing our machine at Pau. With the changes, we have lost and we have gained. The new front elevator steers much better than the old one used to do. There is much more pressure on the underside. We can see the cloth bulging up between the ribs. With the curvature closer to the rear, the centre of pressure is farther back. This makes the ride far more steady, but it means that we are less able to counter-act the effects of a sudden fall.

Prometheus walked through the forest, in the thick of the trees.

Sharing with Man would be no loss to the gods. They should have provided Man with fire of their own volition. Well, sometimes, one has to nudge the gods in the right direction. They will probably be happy when they see what Mankind can accomplish. If not, then we will defy them. All Mankind will be happy to see what fire will enable us to do. Why shouldn't they be, after all? Why shouldn't the secrets of the world be ours to explore?

He was very close to the sleeping-place of the others. His fingers gripped the torch, and he felt like holding it up and waiving it, but he decided not to. It was too early in the evening to go and speak to them. Fire would attract more attention when the world was completely dark.

He decided to wait until nightfall in a cave.

Warp control. Easy on the adjustment. Just a bit. Don't like the ups and downs, but an over-adjustment of the front elevator would easily make us dip and spill us into the Kitty Hawk sand.

There is never a shortage of gods.
When Professor Langley failed, Professor Newcomb told the reporters that the Langley failure proved the impossibility of human flight.
When one professor fails, we turn to another.

Leonardo sat at a table in the Piazza della Signoria, sipping on his wine, slowly turning over the pages of his notebook. The day's reward was a cup of Antonio's best.
The evening grew darker, but with the candle there was light enough to see.
How was it that man would fly? What kind of apparatus would he need? It was his logic to start every drawing with the essence of Man. Anything added must be an extension of Man as he is.
He turned the pages of his notebook.
Man has his limitations, true enough, but oh what assets too. To reach the greatest heights – to soar up closer to the sun – a man need not be anything more than a man.
He set the wine down and took up the pen, and turned to a blank page of the notebook, dipped the nib in the ink, and started to draw.

At Pau, we have reached a culmination. We are demonstrating our flying machine before the world. Our words are translated into a dozen languages; songs are being written about us; our cap is a fashion item; the hobbled skirt has become a fad; we are successfully demonstrating the world's first practical, piloted, controlled, heavier-than-air flying machine. All of our struggles have led to success but now we are anxious to go home, to see our family and complete our work. A world of work lies waiting for us back home at the bicycle shop.

Prometheus stood at the entrance to the cave. Behind him, deep inside, there was a glow. It was still daylight but he didn't want to leave until it was nightfall. It was too dangerous to be seen until he was ready.
He felt he knew what he had done. It had been building up inside him for a very long time. It was based on the question of what it is to be a man. Surely Man should be the one to answer that. What is Mankind capable of doing? How high and how far can a man's hand reach? How many ways can he employ the gift of fire? Whatever it may be, it will show him what it is to be a man.
The sun was moving behind the mountains. The others would soon be shivering, as the warmth of the sun went down. Prometheus knew where they would be huddled. In a little while, he would emerge from the darkness with his gift.

Now the front elevator again. Just a gentle touch. Too much! Too much! Ease off! The elevator isn't balanced. It wants to keep turning itself when started. It doesn't stop turning when we want it to. Too far on the up-side and then too far on the down-side. Very difficult to give it a delicate movement. Have to over-compensate each time we rise or fall.

Leonardo's pen scratched the page. A line here, a line there. Gradually, a vision began to appear as the ink and the paper were transformed into life itself. A straight line, a curve, a shadow. It was the essence-of-man being mated with the essence-of-machine. There was no room for mythological imaginings. The drawing must be the meeting place of all that he had discovered Man to be, and all that he had found the forces of nature to be, and all of the invention that he could muster that would serve to harness the two together as a man-machine.

From time to time, Leonardo remembered to take a sip of wine. When he had finished the drawing, he wrote a brief, exploratory note. The pen moved across the page, right to left. The perfect mirror of his thoughts.

He eased himself back and gave a sigh and rubbed his hip.

The horses of the engine are functioning perfectly here at Pau. The air is bumpy and there are moments when we do not seem to have full control of our machine and we dip downward for a moment, but we raise the elevator slightly and the ancient string is broken – the one that ties us to the ground– and we soar over the fields and the treetops and the heads of the watchers.

Our machine is a gigantic bird with wings as wide as the imagination can make them, with a future as encompassing as the thoughts of man have scope to develop the entire range of possibilities.

Our machine is as beautiful as at the moment of its conception; our machine is as beautiful as our original idea.

We know what we have done.

Cayley, Maxim, Parsons, Bell, Phillips, Lilienthal, Edison, Ader, Moullinard, Chanute, Langley. All of them have tried to unlock the secret of human flight and all of them have failed. They have invented the internal combustion engine, the rapid-firing gun, the turbine steam engine, the telephone, and many other great inventions, but none of them has found the secret of human flight.

We know what we have accomplished.

We have visited places of stress and strain and breaking-points that others have not imagined. We have encountered whirlpools and eddies and the cross-currents of raging torrents and have kept our footing. We have explored the farthest reaches of science and mathematics and pioneered the beginnings of aeronautics.

The water we swim in; the air we breathe. We have surrounded ourselves with an envelope of creativity.

We have breathed a mist of numbers, theories and concepts until they have pulsed through our veins with the blood from our very own hearts. We have stretched our mind to the farthest reaches of ingenuity. We have been to the farthest places and returned with the secret of how to build the world's first practical, human-carrying, powered and controlled flying machine.

And now there are many who are waiting for a chance to pick our pockets of all that we have achieved. It is possible that profit will be lost to us and credit will be denied, but the fact of our achievement is part of what we are and cannot be altered.

Until others retrace our footsteps and re-visit the places where we have been, no one will ever be able to appreciate what we have accomplished.

The amazing power of the wind. Can't believe it affects the direction as much as it does. Today, the wind is strong at Kitty Hawk. We have always done our gliding in lighter winds.

Flight is the absence of all cares, all worries, all personal relationships that founder on suspicion and doubt and misunderstood motives.
Flight is business partnerships that thrive in harmony, personal relationships that grow in mutual trust, and family – the bedrock on which our achievements have been firmly built.
We have clung with an eagle's talons to the single idea that human flight is possible.

At Pau, our sister-Katharine sits beside us as the wind sings in the rigging and the propellers hum in the breeze and the engine snarls. The people wave as we circle above the fields and the crowds below. The machine is flying well. It is times like these that have always been our goal.

Some days we get to soar. Some days we get to soar under ideal conditions. Some days the wind just lifts the wings and we go skimming along so freely on the element that seemed forbidden for a thousand years.
Our machine is as graceful as a bird as it flies in the sunshine. The white expanse of the surfaces, with the sun shining cheerfully on them, and the dark lines of the ribs make it look like all of the predictions of an airborne sailing-yacht.

Have to use a gentler touch or we're going to crash. The double-surface elevator experiment has to be a mistake. Too much response each time we move the lever. Undulating up and down above the Kitty Hawk sand. We shouldn't have hinged the elevator in the centre. The hinge would be better if it was further ahead. A smaller surface would probably make for better control.

Our machine is a large human bird, circling lazily overhead, making a harsh buzzing sound like that of a mowing-machine as it clips the crops in August in the heat of the harvest afternoon.
Our machine is not only functional, it is beautiful. It has beautiful, white, curving, graceful surfaces. It is perfect for the task that it was designed to do.

Soaring above the crowds and the fields at Pau. Determined to break all records for human achievement in the air. Circling above their heads for as long as it takes to prove what we have accomplished.

We have a few things left to do when we get back to Dayton. We promised our father that we would never fly together, but we would like to think that once – just once, for the short space of an hour – he will allow us to set that promise aside. The Wright Brothers flying together, far above the earth, in the Wright Flyer: a physical manifestation of what has been happening spiritually all along.

We would also like to take our father – Bishop Milton Wright, of the Church of the United Brethren in Christ – up into the air, just once, to let him see how it feels for man to fly.

Eighty-one years old, white hair and blue eyes, soaring over the treetops – Leonardo-like – with his beard blown back in the wind. He has always believed that someday man would find his place in the element of the sky.

He has supported us in everything that we have done.

Flying above the crowds and the fields of Europe. Flying above the fields of all the world. All eyes respond as the white wings catch the sun.

Flying is days that are warm, with a lifting breeze coming in over the Atlantic Ocean making the fabric bulge between the spars with anticipation at the easing of the wings up into the air.

Flying warmed a cold day in mid-December, once, at Kitty Hawk.

We have seen days at Kitty Hawk that would take the breath away. Days when the sun is warm on our faces and the breeze is gentle and strong and invites the world to come flying if it will only dare.

Prometheus hovered at the entrance to the cave. He could only imagine what the gift of fire could do. It would be a whole new era for all of Mankind.

After today, perhaps, there would be no need of the sun.

"There is a monster called Chimaera," Katharine says. "It is composed of all the evils that seem to surround us. It gathers these forces in with the thirst of a sponge. Sheer havoc is its only discernable goal. It can only be combatted by a boy on a flying horse."

Evening in the Piazza della Signoria.

The people of Florence discussed the events that had made the day. There was a glow on every face at every table. It had to be an almost perfect place to be.

Leonardo closed his notebook and moved his fingers over the leather. The light from the candle transmuted the wine. Beside his fore-arm, inside the glass, the candle glowed with a clear and steady flame.

Just make one more tiny adjustment – one small change to a strut or a lever or the tip of a wing – and you will soar above the sand and the waves and the ignorance that has kept you earth-bound. You will look down on all you fly over – at the bench and the battery box and the launch-rail; at your footprints in the sand; at the ice-covered puddles and the wind-blown wrinkles; at the sheds of your camp and Big Kill Devil Hill; at the boats making wakes in the ocean; one more glance before they disappear – as if they are merely the toys of industrious ants.

A man would crouch inside this machine. He would place his feet just so, and his hands just so, and when he was ready, he would nod to the others who are helping him, and they would pull their hands away and release the machine.

The winds of Kitty Hawk will lift you up and carry you, on wings of your own devising, as far and as fast and as high as you have ever dreamed that a human can possibly go. Farther and faster and higher than any Greek god who ever had an unbelievable adventure in the pages of your sister-Katharine's books.

The Flyer is moving well, but control is difficult. She rises to about ten feet and then, when we adjust the rudder, she darts towards the ground. Undulating up and down above the Kitty Hawk sand. We should have practised without the motor. We should have altered the new front elevator before the flight.

"Pegasus trots along the hilltop," Katharine says. "He whinnies into the wind and then he breaks out into a gallop and lengthens out his stride and his wings spread out in the shape of a glorious fan. Then he gathers up his strength – every ounce of power in every muscle of his frame – and launches himself away from the pull of the earth. His hoofs stop pounding and the only sound is the breeze. It is a beautiful sunny day. The clouds are white and fluffy. His wings shine brightly as he soars up into the air."

Every once in a while the Flyer darts for the ground. When we move the elevator a bit, she jerks up way too far. Must be ten or twelve seconds, at least, that we've been in the air. Has to be at least a hundred feet. One hundred and ten feet. Maybe a hundred and twenty feet. The sky above, the Kitty Hawk sand below. The first heavier-than-air, powered, controlled human flight! No idea how far we can go. No time to look around and get a sense of what it means to be taking flight, but there is no doubt now that we are actually flying. Who could deny what we have accomplished? One hundred and twenty feet and we're still in the air!

Three Books

The Wright Brothers: Flight is Possible – a novel

As of 1903, life looked like a fairy-tale for the Wright Brothers. The two worked in harmony as a single creative personality in order to perform one of the most amazingly creative acts in the history of mankind – the invention of a machine which would lift man into the air in fulfilment of an age-old dream: human flight. However, by 1909, the fairy-tale is turning into a nightmare, as circumstances force the two brothers apart – one to Washington and one to France – in order to demonstrate the new wonder-machine to the governments of two countries at the same time, as a means of protecting their patent-secrecy. Facing a world of hostility, indifference, ridicule and disbelief, each lonely brother – Wilbur and Orville – draws strength from the memory of the shared enterprise which led to the successful lift-off at Kitty Hawk, on December 7, 1903.

The Making of Flight is Possible – a reflective journal

This journal records the author's reflections on the process of the crafting of the novel as it evolved through the stages of planning, writing, editing and polishing. It constitutes an effort to be as conscious as possible of the process whereby the single idea that suggested the topic of the novel was expanded into a complex work of art. Topics range from the nuts and bolts of novel-building to the nature of the novel as an art-form.

Planning Flight is Possible – a planning notebook

During the writing of the novel, the author kept a hand-written notebook which records the day-by-day development of the novel as it found its shape and style. The notebook – now in print form – reveals how a vast cluster of thoughts was sifted, selected, structured and polished into novel-form.

The Project

Together, this novel, journal and notebook comprise the seventh installment in an on-going novel-writing project in which the author is exploring the concept of form and meaning in the novel, and of the novel as a form of expression in the 21st Century. All of the published journals and notebooks are available for free download at www.johnpassfield.ca.

About the Author

John Passfield was born in St. Thomas, Ontario, Canada, and continues to reside in Southern Ontario, near Cayuga, with his family. He is interested in exploring the development of the novel as an art-form, and has written over twenty novels, twenty planning notebooks and twenty journals in his search for a form for the poetic novel of our time.

Novels by John Passfield

Grave Song
The Agony of Robert Chisholm

Jumbo
P. T. Barnum's Greatest Creation

Pinafore Park
The Swan Boat Incident

Water Lane
The Pilgrimage of Christopher Marlowe

Rain of Fire
The Ordeal of Conductor Spettigue

Victoria Day
The Fabric of the Community

The Wright Brothers
Flight is Possible

Leni Riefenstahl
The Valley of the Shadow

Babe Ruth
Out of the Park

Raskolnikov
Murder with an Axe

Death Day
The Apology of Sergei Eisenstein

Albert Einstein
Wonder

Geoffrey Chaucer
Canterbury Bound

Ospringe
A Visit with Grandad

Pompeii
Vesuvius Dominus

Beethoven
The Ninth Immersion

Job
The Cornerstone of the Universe

Bethune
The Only Person Alive in the World

Terry Fox
Somewhere the Hurting Must Stop

Lord and Lady Macbeth
Full of Scorpions Is My Mind

Cyril Passfield
Out West

Glenn Gould
Light and Dark

Emily Brontë
More Myself Than I

See www.johnpassfield.ca for publishing information.

In Search of Form and Meaning: Journals by John Passfield

Each journal is a day-by-day record of the complex process that a writer undergoes while crafting a work of art. It records the largest decisions, of structure and theme, and the smallest decisions, such as the choice of one word over another, and the constant interaction between the two. Each journal is a record of a writer's reflection on the craft of novel-writing.

The Making of Grave Song

The Making of Jumbo

The Making of Pinafore Park

The Making of Water Lane

The Making of Rain of Fire

The Making of Victoria Day

The Making of Flight is Possible

The Making of The Valley of the Shadow

The Making of Out of the Park

The Making of Murder with an Axe

The Making of Death Day

The Making of Wonder

The Making of Canterbury Bound

The Making of Ospringe

The Making of Vesuvius Dominus

The Making of The Ninth Immersion

The Making of The Cornerstone of the Universe

The Making of The Only Person Alive in the World

The Making of Somewhere the Hurting Must Stop

The Making of Full of Scorpions Is My Mind

The Making of Cyril Passfield: Out West

The Making of Glenn Gould: Light and Dark

The Making of Emily Brontë: More Myself Than I

See www.johnpassfield.ca for publishing information.

The Novel as an Art-Form:
Planning Notebooks by John Passfield

Each planning notebook is a printed version of the hand-written notebook which records the planning, writing, editing and polishing of each novel. Each notebook is an attempt to record, understand, and organize the vast cluster of thoughts which occur as one grapples with the various levels of organization which a clear yet complex work of art demands.

Planning Grave Song

Planning Jumbo

Planning Pinafore Park

Planning Water Lane

Planning Rain of Fire

Planning Victoria Day

Planning Flight is Possible

Planning The Valley of the Shadow

Planning Out of the Park

Planning Murder with an Axe

Planning Death Day

Planning Wonder

Planning Canterbury Bound

Planning Ospringe

Planning Vesuvius Dominus

Planning The Ninth Immersion

Planning The Cornerstone of the Universe

Planning The Only Person Alive in the World

Planning Somewhere the Hurting Must Stop

Planning Full of Scorpions Is My Mind

Planning Cyril Passfield: Out West

Planning Glenn Gould: Light and Dark

Planning Emily Brontë: More Myself Than I

See www.johnpassfield.ca for publishing information.

www.ingramcontent.com/pod-product-compliance
Lightning Source LLC
Chambersburg PA
CBHW070045120526
44589CB00035B/2322